FICTION IN FILMS
FILMS IN FICTION

FICTION IN FILMS
FILMS IN FICTION

the making of new english india

S. SREETILAK

Viva Books

New Delhi | Mumbai | Chennai | Kolkata | Bengaluru | Hyderabad | Kochi | Guwahati

Publisher's note

First Published 2015
Reprint 2017, 2024

Viva Books Private Limited

- 4737/23, Ansari Road, Daryaganj, New Delhi 110 002
  Tel. 42242200, 23258325, 23283121, Email: vivadelhi@vivagroupindia.net
- 76, Service Industries, Shirvane, Sector 1, Nerul, Navi Mumbai 400 706
  Tel. 27721273, 27721274, Email: vivamumbai@vivagroupindia.net
- Megh Towers, Old No. 307, New No. 165, Poonamallee High Road, Maduravoyal
  Chennai 600 095 Tel. 23780991, 23780992, Email: vivachennai@vivagroupindia.net
- B-103, Jindal Towers, 21/1A/3 Darga Road, Kolkata 700 017
  Tel. 22816713, Email: vivakolkata@vivagroupindia.net
- 194, First Floor, Subbramma Chetty Road, Basavanagudi, Bengaluru 560 004
  Tel. 26607409, Email: vivabangalore@vivagroupindia.net
- 101-102, Moghal Marc Apartments, 3-4-637 to 641, Narayanguda, Hyderabad 500 029
  Tel. 27564481, Email: vivahyderabad@vivagroupindia.net
- First Floor, Beevi Towers, SRM Road, Kaloor, Kochi 682 018
  Tel. 0484-2403055, 2403056, Email: vivakochi@vivagroupindia.net
- 232, GNB Road, Beside UCO Bank, Silpukhuri, Guwahati 781 003
  Tel. 0361-2666386, Email: vivaguwahati@vivagroupindia.net

www.vivagroupindia.com

ISBN: 978-81-309-0401-6

Published by Vinod Vasishtha for Viva Books Private Limited, 4737/23 Ansari Road, Daryaganj, New Delhi 110 002.

Printed and bound at Replika Press, Kundli, Sonepat, Haryana.

To my parents

Contents

List of Illustrations

Foreword

An argument that has been rather slow to persuade those who know English is about its power to influence increasingly larger sections of Indians. While officially four to five per cent of Indians "know" English, we know for a fact that English-enabled goods, services, and values have been reaching our country's remotest corners and beyond them to influence nearly everyone's life on a daily basis. English in India covers mental and geographical distances, bridges rural–urban divides, and allows more material means than before that articulate and negotiate such distances and divisions. Happily or otherwise, ideas of modernity, rather than modernity itself, seem to be reaching and reaching out to those – and their numbers are ever increasing – who never seem to have enough of one (English) in order to be able to have the other (modernity). When such social and cultural definitions depend on actual or virtual English, we ought to study it from perspectives other than merely departmental. *Fiction in Films, Films in Fiction* is a bold attempt in precisely this direction. It is the first-ever study of the Indian English film; it studies some of these films in apposition to Indian English fiction, and in so doing, it draws a fairly accurate picture of the *social life* of English, a life whose politics and sociology far exceed the curricular demands of Indian English classrooms.

S. Sreetilak's venture, therefore, is extraordinary; it puts two large domains of English India in contexts that engage and sustain both as "products" that emanate from a corporate, liberalized economy. English fiction and English film in India, argues Sreetilak, seem to "answer each other", the one not only responding alongside the other, but both "answering together to something outside themselves". The nature and extent of such "correspondences" form the subject of this book, which carries sustained discussions of, and commentaries on, more than a dozen Indian English films and stories. It also provides some illustrations and reproductions of prints, covers, and cartoons of Indian English "crossings" and musings on the new culture of English India of the late 1980s through the early years of the present century.

The meatier part of Sreetilak's book selectively reads our English films and stories to show that they record not so much the lives of the people who largely use English, but the life of English India. I am biased favourably towards this idea and argument not least because it can be easily seen everywhere from private lives to professional circles here and abroad. The circles of English use (and abuse) are fast widening, witness the surreptitious and illegal cellphone photography and the nationwide popular response to English-dominated quiz programmes aired on primetime TV. From cooking to terror to baby-sitting to everyday messaging, India has been rediscovering ways of harnessing English to contribute to our GDP. Among Sreetilak's examples that help us see the large sweep of our English sociality is a novel, *Corridor*, whose pages depict graphically the English fortunes of our country still resisting all out corporatisation. Few of us will fail to recognise its titular metaphor. Who hasn't walked a corridor without hoping to reach larger, roomier spaces?

Whether those spaces will indeed be roomier here, or abroad, is moot. Questions, again, might further engage students and fans of Indian English films, much as they had engaged those who inaugurated the writing and reading of Indian English fiction, whether English is really an Indian language, or how Indian is our sensibility when we respond to things English. Isn't that alone a truly magnificent prospect?

K. Narayana Chandran
Professor of English
The University of Hyderabad

CHAPTER I

Introduction

Indian English Fiction and Indian English Film: Some Correspondences

STUDIES of fiction and film generally tend to follow two familiar, if predictable, directions. Either one studies the "fiction-into-film phenomenon", or one tries to read films *as* fiction. The arguments of this book, however, take neither of these directions because the subject here is Indian English. In my view, this is very important because Indian English fiction itself has emerged not so long ago, and Indian English film is fast emerging as a distinct genre. How are these two popular genres *correspondent*, beyond the obvious similarity that both are in English?

I shall assume that both fiction and films in Indian English emerge as *correspondent* phenomena. The reason I assume this is that, however fascinating the two genres themselves are, my chief interest is in English – rather, the *social life of English* as reflected by, and presented in, Indian English fiction and films. The term *correspondences*, in the sense I have used it, requires a brief explanation. The relation of Indian English fiction and Indian English films can be explained as a mutually sustained and sustaining activity of "co-responding", that is, "answering" each other – the one not only "responding alongside" the other, but both of them "answering together" to something outside themselves. In other words, this book is a study of the interaction between the two genres and also of their joint responses to the Indian English culture in general, to the making of which they have contributed in no small measure.

HOLLYWOOD FILMS AND INDIAN FILMS

English movies produced in Hollywood have always charmed the middle-class urban audience in India. Hollywood kept the denizens of the city entertained with images of what they aspired for: fashions, affluence, liberal attitudes, smart living, etc. Those who could understand English films found in them things worth emulation, and prided themselves in this privilege of being able to share something "international". Through the 1960s and 1970s, the interest in English films grew in theatres throughout India. The Morning Show produced the "gentlemen" and "ladies" of urban India. Gregory Peck, Marilyn Monroe, Sean Connery, Greta Garbo et al. became household names for the upper middle-class India. Famous characters like Laurel and Hardy, Charlie Chaplin's tramp, Robin Hood and Sinbad the Sailor animated the imagination of the "English" India and were a formative influence on a whole post-independence generation of Indian youth.[1] The Hollywood heroes John Wayne, Gary Cooper and Kirk Douglas, and pop-singers and bands like Elvis Presley, Frank Sinatra, Cliff Richards, the Beatles and Abba were worshipped as idols (Bhatt 3). Everyone tried to sound knowledgeable about Hollywood, its films, stories, actors and actresses. Very few among them really saw all Hitchcock movies, but the Hitchcockian paradigm of gruesome fantasy and suspense permeated the popular Indian English mind. It is not quite surprising, therefore, to find the footprints of Hitchcock's *Vertigo* in a Satyajit Ray story called "Ratanbabu and That Man", a story Ray himself has translated into English.[2]

Through the 1960s the Hindi movies initiated a trend of sight-seeing thrill and entertainment by taking the viewers abroad. The values and characters they portrayed were enviably un-Indian, and unmistakeably English, their titles so loudly indicative of this trend: *A Night in London*, *An Evening in Paris* and *Love in Tokyo*. English titles for Indian films have continued this trend both as invitation and approbation of the values so "dear" to Indians because they are foreign and exotic. We shall see more about this trend later. The late 1970s and early 1980s saw the mushrooming of film clubs and screening of both English and English-subtitled movies from the West in almost all major cities and small towns in India. English films thus became an important channel for cultural imports. Mahesh Bhatt, one of India's renowned filmmakers, reminisces his generation's experience of Hollywood films thus:

> It was here in the darkness [of the movie halls] that the windows to the United States opened for people like me and my generation. It was through this big screen that one got a glimpse of what the American Dream was all about. Hollywood created a thirst in millions of Indians, some of whom later became part of Bollywood and today are entertaining millions of Indians. Hollywood also shaped our way of life and our way of thinking. It bled into our day-to-day life, our clothes, our speech patterns, our very dreams. (3–4)

Hollywood exercised a formative influence on Indian cinema as well. There have been very interesting variations in the presentation of "English content" in Hindi and other Indian language films. In early Hindi cinema, a westernised and English-speaking character represented everything un-Indian, perhaps all western, and therefore, evil. A man wearing a suit, speaking English with some affectation, and smoking a pipe on the screen was invariably a villain, smuggler, or an abductor. Pran and Ajit usually played the arch-villain roles with anglicised gestures and poses. The hero and heroine stuck strictly to the "tradition" and kept the western manners at a safe distance. English trappings were also characteristic of the "temptress", who smoked and wore western outfits. Roles played by Helen, and some racy numbers of Asha Bhonsle carrying English terms of endearment, are the best examples of such representation.

The Indian cinema of continuing post-globalisation displays exactly the opposite trend. It projects westernisation as desirable and positive. "Englishness" no longer suggests villainy or sabotage, but appears to be the sought-after quality of a modern and contemporary hero(ine). Films like *Dilwale Dulhaniya Le Jayenge, Pardes, Kabhi Khushie Kabhi Gham, Dil Chahta Hai, Kaante, Boom, Kal Ho Na Ho* and *Kabhi Alvida Naa Kehna*, all have an unmistakeable American or European ambience and characters with entirely international airs, who retain their Indian-ness only in the Hindi they speak. Except in very specially cast and designed "period" movies (*Lagaan*, for example), the cast of characters, especially the young protagonists, are shown to be extremely fluent and comfortable speakers of English. Some of them are "sent" to English Schools in the city or abroad (*Kabhi Khushie Kabhi Gham*). Other films, like *Mohabbatein*, pay lip service to *parmpara* and court western education, manners and morals. This shift in the "manner" of Indian cinema can only be read against the backdrop of the culture of English in the country.

Another significant contribution to the social scene of English has been the periodic screening of activist films and documentaries in India's metropolitan cities. The leading name in this category is Anand Patwardhan's. Patwardhan has been making documentaries on political, social and developmental issues since the mid 1970s. His films are in English, but when telecast on the national network, the voice-over in Hindi and regional languages ensures wider interest in films with a studied pan-Indian-English bias and political concern. Patwardhan's documentary realism and serious socio-political messages have undoubtedly influenced both regional films and Indian English films, although Hindi films like *Bombay* and *Sarfarosh* might seem independent takes on the city and communalism with no reference to Patwardhan's *Bombay, Our City* (1985) and *In the Name of God* (1992). The treatment of bold and alternative sexualities in Indian films may not owe anything directly to Patwardhan's *Father, Son and Holy War* (1995), but the film leaves no doubt regarding the educated Indian English attitude towards patriarchal power and macho prowess, very correctly condemned or ridiculed, in Indian English fiction and films of the 1990s.

THE HISTORY OF CORRESPONDENCE

Historically, there has been a long but sporadic regard for each other between Indian English fiction and cinema. Many of the early novels were made into films, both in English and Indian languages. It seems necessary to narrate briefly the run-up to the Indian English films and their establishment as a genre in the more recent times. This is required partly to visualise the body of sporadic Indian English films as a single phenomenon, and also because no such survey is currently available. My list will exclude films that were dubbed into English, documentaries and films that are either very obscure or clearly fall outside the focus of this book. The films that stick to the general theme of the life of Indians either here or abroad, and that also present in some detail the situations of Indians using English as the primary medium of communication, have been included.

One of the first fiction-into-film instances was K. A. Abbas's *Two Leaves and a Bud* (1952), which was a film adaptation of Mulk Raj Anand's novel of the same name. R. K. Narayan's *The Guide* was filmed by Vijay Anand in 1965.[3] The same year a different English version was released in the USA directed by Tad Danielewski. In Kannada, T. S. Nagabharana made a film *Banker Margayya* (1983) based on Narayan's *The Financial Expert*. In the silent era, the better Indian films used to have English subtitles with an eye on the foreign market. According to the *Encyclopaedia of Indian Cinema* (OUP, 1999), from 1932 to 1993 there have been at least 64 sound feature films in English. The early productions include Himanshu Rai's *Song of Serpent* (1933) and Madhu Bose's *Court Dancer* (1941). In the 1960s, the Bombay-born producer Ismail Merchant introduced various India-related issues into international filmmaking in English. He was also the first Indian producer to enjoy success in the English-speaking world. With the American director James Ivory, he formed a successful combine that made films like *The Householder* (1963), *Shakespearewallah* (1965), *Autobiography of a Princess* (1975) and *Heat and Dust* (1983). They were joined in their ventures by the novelist and scriptwriter Ruth Prawer Jhabvala, who wrote the scripts for all these movies.

The Householder tells the story of the frictions of an unstable marriage. It shows the young generation of the 1960s beginning to feel uneasy about the inherited ideas of an "arranged marriage". *Shakespearewallah* places the old English-ruled India in contrast with the new independent society. This black-and-white film is the story of a struggling English troupe touring India to stage Shakespeare plays. *Shakespearewallah* highlights the transitional phase where the popularity of the theatre waned and cinema replaced it as the people's source of entertainment. *Autobiography of a Princess* takes the viewer through the reminiscences of one of the erstwhile Indian royalty, now an exile in London. The screenplay was again by Jhabvala, and the film used footage of real maharajas shot by Merchant while on a visit to Jodhpur. Jhabvala adapted the screenplay of the film *Heat and Dust* from her own novel. In the colonial India of the 1920s, the wife of an English civil servant starts a scandalous romance with a Nawab, and is consequently ostracised by the British community. The narrative unfolds through the reconstruction of the lady's affair by a descendant of hers, who visits India 50 years later. *The Perfect Murder* is a murder mystery adapted by Zafar Hai from a novel by H. R. F. Keating. Although not treated here as Indian English films as such, these films are important precursors to them. They are better qualified by the label "Anglo-Indian", a category that will include *A Passage to India*, Attenborough's *Gandhi*, etc.

The film that inaugurated what we term the Indian English film is Aparna Sen's *36 Chowringhee Lane* (1981). Inspired by European models, this film is about an aged Anglo-Indian lady, Violet Stoneham, working as an English teacher in a Calcutta school. Parallel to her story is portrayed an educated and urbanised generation of young Bengalis, who exploit the lady's generosity and kind ways. These people are shown to embrace western manners and morality in the way any generation goes after its own "in" things. "*36 Chowringhee Lane* is a film ... by English-speaking people, of English-speaking people but ... not necessarily *for* all English-speaking people" (Vaidyanathan 109).

My Beautiful Laundrette (1985), scripted by Hanif Kureishi, deals with the life of Asian immigrants in Britain. Their integration into the mainstream is troubled because of the difficult racial relations. He says: "We decided the film was to have gangster and thriller elements, since the gangster film is the form that corresponds most closely to the city, with its gangs and violence. And the film was to be an amusement, despite its references to racism, unemployment and Thatcherism" (125). The themes Kureishi presents here are a recurrent concern in many later films, that is, the "NRI" sub-category of Indian English films. In one way or another, all the movies of this group deal with the aftermath of Indian families' displacement from the subcontinent to various parts of the western world. The familiar elements of the NRI world picture are: the mixed identity of the second-generation immigrants, their vacillation between traditional and modern values and moralities, nostalgia, the lack of nostalgia, success and other results of expatriation. Mira Nair's *Mississippi Masala* (1994) reproduces the travails of an uprooted Indian family struggling to cope with a succession of societies. Exiled from Uganda by the dictator Idi Amin, they end up in Mississippi as the owners of a motel. The young daughter Mina falls in love with a black American and decides to make him her partner, much against the traditionally-minded parents' wishes. The story of an Indian community in Canada, *Masala* (1994), directed by Srinivas Krishna, can also be slotted in the same family of films. The protagonist here is in a desperate attempt to acclimatise himself in the new Canadian soil.

Many Indian English directors chose to set the films themselves in India for a few years between the first occurrence and the later spate of "NRI" films. Notable among them is Dev Benegal, whose collaboration with the writer Upamanyu Chatterjee made two remarkable contributions to the set of Indian English films: *English, August* (1994) and *Split Wide Open* (1999), which explore two contrastive landscapes of modern India and comment on the flip side of the nation's progress. Agastya Sen, a fresh IAS recruit, is posted in a remote, inhospitable small town called Madna, where life turns out for him to be a far cry from the urban luxuries the likes of him have all the way been used to. Agastya's anglicised nickname "August" gives the film its title.

Split Wide Open is a critical take on the Indian metropolis of the post-globalisation era. An audacious TV talk show "Split Wide Open" is determined to expose the dark secrets of the city elite's sex lives. Against this backdrop is set the career of the youngster K. P., orphaned, but up and coming because of the English education he receives from a benevolent missionary. This film is remarkable for its harsh naturalism and unusual candour verging on outspokenness, two qualities which have eluded commercial mainstream cinema in India. This film, again, is developed from a short story by Upamanyu Chatterjee. One of the welcome features of Indian-made English movies is that they break the stigma attached to subjects of sexuality, about which their Indian language counterparts are shy, silent, or patently outspoken. Mira Nair's *Kama Sutra, A Tale of Love* (1996) presents bluntly the sexual intrigues of a medieval court. Deepa Mehta's *Fire* (1996) presents lesbian love between two sister-in-laws in a traditional household.

With Nagesh Kukunoor's *Hyderabad Blues* (1998), the NRI-oriented tales made a return to the screen. Varun, an NRI, returns from the US to his hometown Hyderabad, and his parents begin attempts to arrange a marriage for him. But the hero hardly shares his parents' ideas about marriage and ties the knot with a girl of another caste whom he loves. The entire film is told from a comic angle and was an instant hit with the urban audiences who immediately identified themselves with the characters. In the 1990s, when the Indian economy was liberalised and the society seemed agog with new consumer products and services, the aspirations and anxieties of the city youth were the same as those of the hero of this film. Piyush Dinkar Pandya's *American Desi* (2001) is another illustration of the immigrant Indian's cultural perplexity. Born and brought up in America, Krishnagopal Reddy chooses to embrace the host culture and values, firmly rejecting the Indian culture as preserved and practised by his parents in his home. Towards the more conventional and nostalgic Indian roommates of his, Kris's (he prefers the Americanised short form) attitude is dismissive. Yet at the end of the film, we find him a more traditional man matched with his Indian girlfriend. Revathi's *Mitr, My Friend* (2001) has a theme structured similarly to the basic story line of most "crossover" films. Its basic formula is a rebellious teen-aged daughter versus traditional parents, and America versus India, by extension. The standard hero(ine) of the films of this category is the "American Born Confused Desi", the phrase being the title of a movie released in 1999.

In the same year another film came out that compares well with *My Beautiful Laundrette*. That was *East Is East* directed by Damien O'Donnell. Starring Om Puri as a Pakistani merchant in the UK, it portrays George Khan's tussle with his half-white children as he tries to raise them as traditional Muslims. They, however, stubbornly refuse to be groomed as obsolete patriarchs and have their own ways, leaving their father a shattered man whose efforts to "Islamise" them have come to nought. Different from this type, *Mystic Masseur* (2001) traces the story of a failed writer of Indian origin in Trinidad, a place of considerable Indian concentration. This was the film version of Sir V. S. Naipaul's first novel adapted under the direction of Ismail Merchant. Ganesh, the hero, abandons his frustrated literary ambitions to take up his ancestral trade of a healer, which earns him quite some fortune and fame.

The onslaught of western culture through English education and various media in the more contemporary period has not really diminished the urban Indian's regard for traditional customs, religions and belief, but has only intensified his/her desire to preserve them. In *Monsoon Wedding* (2001) by Mira Nair, we find a wealthy Punjabi family's eager commitment to the age-old ideas of kinship and marriage while continuing to thrive amid modernity. The merry celebrations of marriage are marred by the revelations about a paedophile uncle's abuse of his dead brother's daughter. While extolling the buoyant air of the new upper middle class of India, *Monsoon Wedding* also makes a blunt point about some of the murky realities often suppressed behind the facade of the family.

In 2002 Indian English cinema briefly digressed from its "crossover" tendencies and began to pay some attention to domestic themes through the following films: *Mr and Mrs Iyer* by Aparna Sen, *Let's Talk* by Ram Madhvani, *Everybody Says I'm Fine* directed by Rahul Bose and V. K. Prakash's *Freaky*

Chakra (2003). An orthodox Tamil Brahmin Meenaxi Iyer, probably on her first journey home without her husband, travels alone in a bus with her baby. A photographer Jehanghir Choudhuri (Raja), a Muslim, introduced to her by a mutual friend, is given the charge of looking after the lady and the child through their journey. Communal riots break out, and a gang of extremists on a murderous hunt for Muslims waylays the bus. In spite of her prejudices, Meenaxi lies to the murderers that Raja and she are man and wife, and saves his life. Meenaxi and Raja represent the class of Indians whose English education and upbringing have helped them transcend sectarian identities and uphold liberal and humanist values. The film places them in contrast to that India – the uneducated and misguided communalists – whose mindset has remained impervious to the worthy ideals of modernity.

Hindi cinema, which often represents Indian cinema as a whole, appears to have many constraints that disallow a certain maturity for films. Its market base, comprising mainly people of average or no education, requires it to be simplistic on "show-and-tell" terms, or be predictable and invariably uncritical. Some exceptions of recent vintage, each incomparably wide and differently nuanced, are *Maqbool* (2003), *Ek Hasina Thi* (2003), *Iqbal* (2005), *Mixed Doubles* (2006), and *Omkara* (2006). Although we cannot establish the truth of circumambient influence, I shall argue that these screenplays have benefited from Indian English films and address much the same audience at which these Hindi films have also been targeted. The audience would hardly tolerate any defamiliarisation of the plot archetypes, let alone appreciate experimentation. At the same time, the highly educated elite audience nurse contemptuous sentiments towards the popular flicks. They invariably turned to the more cerebral parallel cinema of India and "art" films from all over the world. The Indian English films, though not as intellectual as the parallel films of some Indian languages, are more serious and realistic in subject and treatment. In Ram Madhvani's *Let's Talk*, a housewife gets pregnant as a result of an adulterous affair. The film unfolds as various reactions of her husband as imagined by her, should she confess to him her infidelity. Resembling a stage play, *Let's Talk* offers a mature discussion of marital fidelity in the present-day metropolitan life.

Rahul Bose, a familiar face in Indian English films, turned director with *Everybody Says I'm Fine* released in 2002. It is a film about the well-kept secrets of elite Bombay and the hypocritical masks that cover ugly faces. A movie critic of the *LA Weekly*, Jon Strickland, finds the film different in this way: "*Everybody Says I'm Fine* presents the face of a young, urban westernised Bombay where everyone speaks English and every trace of Indian exoticism has been consciously removed." A reviewer Roger Ebert from *Chicago Sun-Times* similarly perceives this film to be of a different breed: "The movie was shot in English not for the export market, but for India's domestic English speakers, who tend to be toward the top of the economic scale and are beginning to tire of endless Bollywood mega productions." A young hairdresser Xen, running a posh salon in the city, has the gift of reading people's minds. He gets involved in the lives of regular customers whose thoughts reveal themselves to Xen as he cuts their hair. He manages to help some of them out of their crises in life by his timely interventions.

Freaky Chakra by V. K. Prakash portrays a widow's rediscovery of relationships. It features the resultant emotional turmoil of Mrs Thomas, the widow, and a nineteen-year-old boy who rents a room in her apartment.

Yet another sub-category of the English films ridicules the common delusions, complacencies and moral prejudices of the average Indians. It is here that Kukunoor's *Bollywood Calling*

(2002) and Anant Balani's *Mumbai Matinee* (2003) belong. *Bollywood Calling* is a boisterous pastiche of the incredible sequences and stereotypes of popular Hindi cinema. It is told from the point of view of an American actor who gets a chance to act in an Indian film. The movie prioritises a refined and internationalised sensibility over the layman's love of fantastic and maudlin melodrama. In *Mumbai Matinee*, a marketing professional Debashish Chatterjee is disturbed by the fact that his virginity continues into the thirty-second year of his life. He is determined to lose it at the earliest opportunity. Balani offers a satiric film on the sexual suppression characteristic of the rigid Indian morality. The film also makes fun of the people's tendency to seek exotic alternatives to the real problems of life.

Throughout the nineties, and the early years of this century, there has been a spate of NRI movies. Gurinder Chadha's *Bend It Like Beckham* (2002) and *Bride and Prejudice* (2004), with their stupendous success, earned the Indian English film international name and popularity. The theme in *Bend It Like Beckham*, as usual, is the life of the second generation Indians who are in a quandary over the question of ethnicity and adherence to the host environment. The plot runs like this: the youngest daughter of a Punjabi family in Britain, Jesminder Bahmra, has ambitions of becoming a professional footballer. Her idol is the British soccer celebrity David Beckham. The parents' plans are different from hers – they want her to learn to cook so that she can make a "good" Punjabi bride and get married traditionally as her sister is soon to do. Featuring Beckham himself in a short footage, the film was a whopping blockbuster, with the result that Chadha became one of the richest Asians in the United Kingdom.

Bollywood/Hollywood (2002), directed by Deepa Mehta, more or less repeats the familiar NRI story where an initially rebellious young protagonist eventually accepts the Indian identity by his own or the director's will. The story of *Anita and Me*, directed by Metin Huseyin based on a book by Meera Syal, runs on similar lines. *Leela* (2003) is the story of an Indian academic in an American university where she gets involved with an Indian student much younger than her. Leela's emotional life is rejuvenated as she meets Kris, her young ambivalent admirer. Her husband Nashaad, a famous poet, enters the scene as Leela's acquaintance with Kris takes on an adulterous course. The director of the film is Somnath Sen.

In an interview about his film *Being Cyrus* (2006) actor Saif Ali Khan said: "The first reason why I was involved in it [the film] was because I always wanted to do something in English. . . . I thought to do this film because many of us speak in English in this country and not lots of English films come out of the country. I actually think that everyone really likes watching these films" (*The Hindu*, 24 March 2006).

After fiction, the rise of the genre of English films in India is symptomatic of the growing extent of the influence in the national domain of a linguistic community of English-speaking and English-adoring Indians. This book focuses mainly on the post-1980 fiction and films in Indian English. I have attempted to map the emergent context of English in India, in order to show that the diverse carriers of social comment such as the media, writing and cinema exist like a network, bonded and sponsored by English itself. Evidence, most compelling and unignorable, is everywhere to see if only one carefully looked at the fast-changing "social scene" of Indian cinema. If the sixties and the seventies films prided themselves in the "chaste" titles of either Sanskrit–Persian (*Ankur*, *Aakrosh*, *Bhoomika*, *Utsav*, etc.) or of their modern language descendants, Urdu, Hindi and other Indian languages, (*Deewar*, *Insaaf Ki Taraazu*, *Muqaddar Ka Sikander*, etc.), from the mid nineties, directors and producers of films in regional languages seem to prefer English titles to *desi* ones. It is not as though the Indian filmdom has run out of its thesaural lists, but the makers of films know very well that hard and poetic-sounding Urdu titles no longer pull young crowds in cities and towns. If anything, Hindi remakes of Hollywood commercial movies are better served anyway by other suggestive *English* titles. The advantage film directors/producers have found in this is that an English title can simply cover a multitude of sins (their own, like plagiarism) and uncover a host of others under the aegis of a cultural change of heart and a permissive lifestyle. In a movie with an English title, the lives of our people can legitimately be modern and fashionable to warrant daring western folkways and mores. A recent Malayalam film *4 the People*, directed by Jayaraj (a runaway hit with the same title in Telugu), shows daring cyber-age young men trying to police the society.

"Everyone understands English today," says Honey Irani, the scriptwriter. *Everyone*? Well, it would seem so, from the list I have compiled of a dozen or so Hindi movies all of 2004–2006:

Page Three (Madhur Bhandarkar)
Luck by Chance (Zoya Akhtar)
Take Two (Amit Saxena)
Film Star (Tanuja Chandra)
Raincoat (Rituparno Ghosh)
No Entry (Anees Bazmi)
Run (Jeeva)
Sins (Vinod Pande)
Rewind (Ruchi Narain)
Cabaret (Pooja Bhatt)
Lucky: No Time for Love (Radhika Rao)
Murder (Anurag Basu)
Black (Sanjay Leela Bhansali)

Blackmail (Anil Devgan)
Let's Enjoy (Siddharth Anand Kumar and Ankur Tewari)
Bluffmaster (Rohan Sippy)
Tom, Dick and Harry (Deepak Tijori)
Gangster (Anurag Basu)
Corporate (Madhur Bhandarkar)

Take *Page Three.* Madhur Bhandarkar did quite well for himself with *Chandni Bar* only two years before, but in 2005, his pot-shot at Page-Three culture couldn't have done the trick with a poor *Teesra Panna.*

From the above sketch of the Indian English cinema, we can draw a few critical conclusions. A new class of Indians ("the new Macaulayists"?) has found in it a mode of self-expression by deviating from the increasingly stereotypical Hindi/Indian-language films towards the unconventional content of the English films. Away from India, they have become representative of the cultural situation of the ethnic Indian minority across the English-speaking world. Certain it is that this is one way of disseminating the concept of India among the international community, by providing it visibly and intelligibly in English – a function English writing from the country has been hitherto serving rather awkwardly.

Statistical evidence is that the Indian English film productions have been on the rise in response to national and international success. Again, the expanded scope justifies the inclusion here of films whose country of production was not India, but the USA, the UK (*Bend It Like Beckham*) and sometimes, Canada (e.g. *Masala, Anita and Me*). Similarly, the directors of these films are of non-Indian origin in many cases. I have confidently dispensed with such rigours of nationality and domicile whenever the experience depicted in a film is Indian, and the language of its articulation, English.

THE FUNCTION OF ENGLISH

In an article celebrating the multilingualism of India Shashi Tharoor writes: "Indeed, when two Indians meet abroad, or two educated urban Indians meet in India, unless they have prior reason to believe they have an Indian language in common, the first language they speak to each other is English. It is in English that they establish each other's linguistic identity and then they switch comfortably to another language, or a hybrid depending on the link they have established" (*The Hindu*, 13 Aug 2006).

The linguistic and cultural pluralism of India has favoured the cause of English at the cost of competitors like Hindi and other regional languages. Within no time after the introduction of English into the difficult linguistic configuration of the country, it became the pan-Indian medium through which people of different regional backgrounds could communicate. That it set apart a powerful national elite from the traditional society needs no other proof than the history of modern India. Remarkably, the bifurcation of the nation achieved by English had no drawbacks of a class division, but it was welcome since the emergent class started to import modernity from the West and strived to upgrade India's prospects in terms of international standards. Moreover, to become member of this privileged group was not difficult – a good education (which meant English for all intents and purposes) and assimilation of some values made class migrations into this group widely possible. Over the years this process has consolidated a politically strong, economically well-off and educationally advanced middle class. It is this class that the government and public media first heed to. It has also come to represent the nation and its progress to the world outside.

English is not merely another language among many Indian

languages. It has historical and political pre-eminence over its native fellow-languages. The fraction of English users in India "inevitably comprise[s] the entire leadership of India's economic, industrial, professional, political and social life" (Quirk vii). Does the spread of English mean another addition to the already unmanageable linguistic diversity of this country and further divisions of language and class? The answer is, fortunately, no. In India English worked as an overarching unifier language that made the linguistic diversity more manageable. Describing the importance English came to assume for India, Braj Kachru observes:

> By the 1920s, English had become the language of political discourse, intranational administration, and law, and it was associated with liberal thinking. These roles and such an attitude toward English, maintained its power over local languages even after the colonial period ended. (8)

To estimate the diffusion of English into Indian culture since that, one needs to examine the way it got distributed in the country – chiefly, publications of various kinds in English.

WRITING IN ENGLISH AND THE SOCIETY

The emergence of Indian English fiction in the 1920s was an important event in the history of integration of English into Indian culture. The first group of writers, R. K. Narayan, Mulk Raj Anand, Raja Rao, Kamala Markandaya and Anita Desai, wrote their books in the popular genre of the novel. English up to 1920s was confined into the sporadic nationalistic Indian English poetry of the nineteenth century. With fiction English was proved to have another wider use: for the novel was a popular genre. That other writing – historical, political, journalistic and scientific – existed in English much before the appearance of fiction does not discredit the importance of the inauguration of Indian English fiction. The detachment and neutrality that these non-literary forms of writing demanded can be argued to have emptied them of the intimate experiential involvement in cultural life that only creative writing is capable of.

The life depicted in the early Indian English fiction did not differ much from that in literatures in Indian languages. R. K. Narayan wrote about the Tamils and Kannadigas in the imaginary South Indian town of Malgudi; Anand had for his novels north Indian lower-class life as theme; Raja Rao's preoccupation was with South Indian villages, and metaphysics. In the early works the linguistic make-up of the settings depicted did not include the English language in any central role. That is, the characters of these novels actually would have spoken some other language – Tamil or Hindi or Kannada – if they had been. But somehow the readers felt that the world of English was not very far from the Indian scene if they recalled some English ways of Narayan's Malgudi. The schools, the missionaries, government officials, and characters frequenting clubs are the features that give an "English" colour to this Indian town. These early works displayed a curious multilingualism: the authors wrote in English, but the references, both political and cultural, lay in an Indian language. The mental recreation of the stories, characters and dialogue meant translation of a kind. Indian English novels of the first generation present an interesting case of the language of expression not being the language of experience.

The result of the gap between the languages of the represented and the language of representation, however, was not defective literature. The writer had to enable a foreign language to contain details available in a native language and culture. Raja Rao writes about how he found English adaptable to the Indian context:

> One has to convey in a language that is not one's own, the spirit that is one's own. One has to convey the various shades and omissions of a certain thought movement that looks maltreated in an alien language. I use the word 'alien', yet English is not really an alien language to us. It is the language of our intellectual make-up – like Sanskrit or Persian was before – but not our emotional make-up. We are all instinctively bilingual, many of us writing in our own language and English. We cannot write like the English. We should not. We cannot write only as Indians. We have grown to look at the large world as part of us. Our method of expression has to be a dialect which will some day prove to be as distinctive and colourful as the Irish or the American. Time alone will justify it. (Rao v–vi)

English thus enabled is known as Indian English. Indian English fiction proved that English was most suitable to write about India. On the other hand, literature alone was not responsible for the invention of the new English. The role of non-literary traditions in print form such as newspapers, journals and magazines, which had a wider reach, was pivotal too.

We get only half the picture from studying this adaptation of English to depict Indian life. This evolutionary model needs socio-historical evidences that are tangibly present. Why isn't a study of literary history and history of English publishing enough to explain the roles English has played? We cannot ignore the reformation of lifestyles, the change of attitudes, the redefinition of priorities and the internationalisation of outlook – in short, all the noticeable changes that followed in the wake of English. In other words, what we have to study is the *social life of English.*

The linguist Probal Dasgupta gives a sociological mapping that shows how the response to and utilities of English have varied over the period of its history in this country: "English used to function as an instrument of vertical power, serving the purposes and intentions of an unashamed imperial and master-class" (78). The design behind the British decision to introduce officially and underwrite English education in India was to sow the seeds of admiration in Indian minds for the imperial power, using literary education to build up an attractive image of English literary tradition. "Indians who were initiated to the colonial space of English hoped to acquire the language integratively, as a badge of membership to an enlightened elite" (78–9). But in the recent period, Dasgupta argues, English has turned more an instrument than an integrator. Nevertheless, it is only likely that an instrument for socio-economic, scientific and technological progress would create an affluent elite as the agents and beneficiaries of that progress. The Indian experience of English, its growth into an essential commodity of public life, convinces us that the instrumental and integral uses of English have in fact been coexistent and not exclusive, the first leading to the second.

The social life of English expanded through English dailies, magazines, weeklies and other periodical publications apart from the news and analysis broadcasts of All India Radio English. Four English newspapers have been in existence for more than a hundred years now. They are: *The Times of India* (1850), *The Pioneer* (1865), *Amrita Bazar Patrika* (1868) and *The Hindu* (1878). Apart from newspapers, a series of popular periodicals popularised the English language. Among them are: *The Illustrated Weekly of India, The Imprint, Blitz, Eve's Weekly, India Today, The Week, Outlook, Filmfare, The Cosmopolitan, Femina, Society, Stardust, Businessline*, etc. Through the mid 1980s and 90s the mighty broadcast medium invaded India. It brought numerous television channels that were exclusively or partly in the English language. The globalisation of the Indian national media opened the way for trans-national broadcasters into an English language television market that is potentially the world's largest (Thussu 294). The earliest entrants were the CNN, BBC and the Satellite Television Asian Region (STAR). They were instantly accepted, and in a decade's time, their number increased many folds. The cultural changes brought about by the media revolution of the 1990s may well be regarded as the triumph of English. With their news, information and entertainment channels, the networks united the English-knowing population of India as never before by nationally televising in their virtual medium the disparate as well as common aspects of the middle-class life. From documentary writings to literature, from print publications to electronic media, and from an instrument of progress to a way of life, English penetrated nearly every aspect of urban life. Is English then the true facilitator of all that are grouped under the label "westernisation"?

TWO DISTINCT GENRES OF INDIAN ENGLISH CULTURE

In the last two decades of the previous century, there has been an unprecedented spurt of creativity in English with the "second generation" of English writers producing literature successfully and prolifically. Indian writing in English was internationally represented as *the* literature of India. In the words of Meenakshi Mukherjee, "The growing visibility of English as the preferred language of literature in India seems to be an irreversible process" (183).

The impetus for the large-scale appearance of Indian English novels was certainly the internationally acclaimed *Midnight's Children* (1981) by Salman Rushdie and its subsequent global recognition by the Booker Prize. Importantly, its year of release coincided with that of Aparna Sen's *36 Chowringhee Lane*, a landmark in the history of Indian English films. The writers who hoped to repeat Rushdie's success, and really did, were Amitav Ghosh, Vikram Seth, Rohinton Mistry, Arundhati Roy, Upamanyu Chatterjee, Allan Sealy, Pankaj Mishra, Namita

Gokhale, Amit Choudhuri, Bharati Mukherjee, Shobha De, et al. These writers have one major advantage because of their chosen medium. The thematic scope of their writing excluded the untranslatable specificities of traditional Indian life. They have, therefore, solved for themselves and their readership, the problem of limited, regional intelligibility. (This factor has worked against Indian language literatures being read or recognised at levels beyond the regional even in reasonably good translations.) The English writers' substitutes for the unfamiliar culture-specific subjects were themes of urban life that had been made nationally and internationally identifiable by various media. About the convenience of writing in English Shashi Tharoor observes:

> I write of an India of multiple truths and multiple realities, an India that is greater than the sum of its parts. English expresses that diversity better than any Indian language precisely because it is not rooted in any one region of my vast country. (*The Hindu*, 5 Aug 2001)

On the strength of this national character, if you will, Indian English fiction has become a large literary and academic enterprise aligning with new literatures elsewhere, such as African, Caribbean, Canadian, Australian and ethnic American literatures, and seeking theoretical vindication from critical vogues like postcolonialism and postmodernism.

When their productions multiplied in the 1980s, the Indian English films were still experimental and rather tentative as a medium. Their growth since then has been similar to that of English literature by Indians. Some common attributes of many novels and films in Indian English are, the "NRI" orientation, unconventional themes like bold sexuality and social hypocrisy, parody of the traditional ways of life, and sometimes a sort of elitism and snobbishness that characterise much of Indian English fiction and some poetry – themes that only English allows to discuss neutrally.

Let us examine the similarities of Indian English fiction and films one by one with specific illustrations. Expatriation, to begin with, is a frequent theme in the films and novels. Moreover, expatriation is not merely an intrinsic concern of these works, but a condition also, of their writers and directors. Authors like Amitav Ghosh, Allan Sealy, Rohinton Mistry, Vikram Seth, Gita Hariharan, Amit Choudhuri, Bharati Mukherjee, Shashi Tharoor and Mukul Kesavan have either studied, lived or worked abroad. Filmmakers Mira Nair, Gurinder Chadha and Ismail Merchant straddle India and the West, producing films about the cross-border cultures they inhabit. Nair's *Mississippi Masala*, Chadha's *Bend It Like Beckham* and *Bride and Prejudice*, and Merchant's *Mystic Masseur* deal with the expatriate Indian's struggles and experiences in countries of their residence.

In the second common sub-category should be named films of Aparna Sen, Rahul Bose and Deepa Mehta, and novels of Shobha De, Namita Gokhale and Upamanyu Chatterjee. Their works basically derive from the "complexes" and complexities of Indian middle-class life as it is believed to be led in Indian metros and cities abroad. Inside this circle, De's *Socialite Evenings* and Gokhale's *Paro* share the stories of sexual escapades with Deepa Mehta's *Fire* and Anant Balani's *Mumbai Matinee.* Both attempt a social critique of religion, morals, and traditional folkways and more. The affected lifestyles and hypocrisy of the urban elite are ridiculed, and sometimes mildly appreciated, in *Paro, Socialite Evenings* as well as in Rahul Bose's film *Everybody Says I'm Fine.*

But the cinema here in English, although simultaneous and abreast with the literary counterpart, somehow did not get categorised as a genre on par with fiction. The *Encyclopaedia of Indian Cinema* (OUP, 1995) by Ashish Rajyadhyaksha and Paul Willeman includes no separate entry on English movies made in India. Nevertheless, the fact that these films find acceptance in our country and abroad, and have since only increased in number, leads to an important conclusion: *English has indeed conquered one medium after another of socio-cultural expression, and has spread itself integratively into the literary, academic, political, public and geographical spaces of India.* Beginning with documentary writing, through periodicals and then fiction, English has matured into an integral part of India's cultural landscape. Cinema, it would appear, was the last fortress of our culture to fall, albeit with some initial and perfunctory resistance. Considering the natural growth and substantive presence of the Indian English cinema, a cultural cartography of India need not hesitate to assign to it a decent position alongside Indian English fiction as an emergent and vastly progressive genre.

The closeness of English fiction and films in India is by no means accidental. The ground of comparison between them must extend beyond this evident common subscription to the English language. Their common domain is not merely the abstract entity of language, but the concrete cultural reality whose properties they reflect. Both spring from, and are nurtured by, *the social life of English.* The English fiction of our generation concerns itself with stories of the vastly growing urban India, where characters and themes display, in a trans-novelistic manner, a uniformity of cultural field from which they originate. The features of this field are westernised lifestyles, and apparently liberal and secular outlook, individualism, affluence, and above all, the English language. There is no disparity between the languages of expression and experience as in the early English fiction. English is inseparable from the life represented; to complete the cultural references no mental translation is required. The Indian English film, differing on no account in terms of its social source, can easily be found to be repeating the same function with a change of medium for the cinematic. Unlike the popular Indian-language films, their characters are mostly realistic, more lifelike. They are "realistic" to the extent that the English-living middle class of India is recognisable, homogenised and perceived as an entity. The social matrix of English is parental to these fictions and films. In other words, the conditions, means, circumstances and patterns of their participation in the social life of English make Indian English fiction and Indian English film correspondent genres.

* * *

ENGLISH AND CORPORATE INDIA

To return to *correspondence* once again: both Indian fiction and film in English "answer together" to something outside themselves, which I propose to call the *social life of English*. We shall look at some select domains of social life to which English is the facilitating language. There are significant links between English, or rather, the English sub-culture and the rise of "corporate" India in the 1990s. A detailed historical analysis is hardly required to see at least some salient features of India's "new" English, a language whose role in building and cementing corporate empires all through our country is unmistakeable. For example, when Arjun Appadurai characterises the dual function of globalisation in terms of increased migration across countries and cultures, and the rise of the new electronic media, he does not specifically trace these phenomena to English. In one sense he has left out the obvious. "Electronic mediation" and "mass migration" could not effectively have crossed borders and closed gaps without English (4). Transnational identities require a transnational language to make them in the first place. India's English is, and has been, that effective binder of loyalties and traditions to new opportunities and modernities. English, in other words, enables the members of Appadurai's disintegrating "nation-states" to inhabit a "world in motion". It is the unacknowledged adhesive of the postnational world.

Even when we do not care to see English playing this crucial role within, across, and without India in a global scene, it silently does. For example, *Lagaan* (2001), whose phenomenal success here and abroad, in one basic sense, is all thanks to English: British India, cricket, cantonment, the land levy (*lagaan*), colonial history and politics, nationalist pride, even a little anti-English jingoism and camaraderie. English is the medium of its description and contextualisation that alone made possible the international comprehension of *Lagaan*. The surroundings and the backdrop against which the outside world appreciated the film were made of English. This other English, which is different from the language and reality of English life portrayed in the film – the medium – is the one that carries its message successfully in equal measure to both the Indian Prime Minister and his British counterpart. Revathi Krishnaswamy, who has written on the "immigration" of this Bollywood classic in a globalised economy, again, lists everything except English while explaining its success:

> *Lagaan* captured the popular imagination by powerfully yoking cricket with the Indian nation. The film's use of cricket as a metaphor for colonial relations ensures that there will be no ugly exposures of imperial exploitations. Its playful appeal to the spirit of sportsmanship was applauded by both Vajpayee and Tony Blair. (24)

What English has been doing over the last two decades to make our economic liberalisation possible will be clearer, if we sketched here the social life of English in India. To begin with, our schools and colleges are reinventing English for purposes other than those for which it was once famed: education. English, in other words, began to be seen as "a social marker, a password for an entry into the higher echelons of social and cultural power", according to a writer in *The Hindu* Supplement for 4 April 2000 (A. R. Venkatachalapathy). The same children have now grown up to acquire social skills rather than sound knowledge. Reports from across the country tell us of the mushrooming of English teaching shops. Here is one sample:

> Not surprisingly, it's boom time for the many English-speaking institutes. . . . And if you thought they teach only English, think again. Many of them are now doubling as personality grooming centres, training starry-eyed girls from villages in the art of netting NRI husbands. (*Outlook*, April 21, 2003, 58)

In 2000 sprang up NELTS, the National English Language Testing Service, in Hyderabad, under the joint auspices of the Central Institute of English and Foreign Languages (CIEFL) and a publisher of school–college textbooks, Orient Longman Limited. The question this Service posed to anyone who could read their advertisement was: "How good is your English?" About 20 cities across India were identified in the advertisement as centres where the NELTS proposed to hold the test. One paid Rs 400 to obtain a certificate of proficiency in English "awarded", according to the advertisement, by the CIEFL Hyderabad. "The certificate", assured the ad, "will give you a winning edge in today's competitive environment."

Edge or no, the competition for English is real, as David Crystal's *English as a Global Language* (1997) attests. 50 years after the country became free, English should still claim to be all these for our people depending upon their proficiency or lack of it: First, Second or Foreign Language. "Corporate" India, however, is at pains to widen the circles of English influence for business purposes.[4] It is important to make people literate in English to give them loans, front- and back-office jobs, accommodation, photo-identity, passports, membership in societies and unions, etc. There are of course loud cries of protest against westernisation and English-speaking secularists, but one should take a long view of this mandatory frowning. The opposition from certain conservative political sections against modern values is, on closer look, an increasing demand *for* English, rather than against it. The hardcore *swadeshi* advocates are really asking for more share of the English cake, to be eaten and had, at their leisure. In her "Call Centre Drawl", Sagarika Ghose surveys this part of the English scene thus:

> It could even be argued that the fear of westernisation is quite unfounded because most people grow out of MTV and fiercely return to their bharatiya roots (and the Upanishads) as soon as they hit forty. Just look at Protima Bedi . . . . An elaborate hypocrisy surrounds English as politicians mouth the virtues of Hindi yet rush to English language TV studio, for acceptance from the babalog. (Ghose 8)

That the circle of English has been widening pretty fast in the last decade is evident from the hurried and, sometimes unusually varied, patterns of its teaching and learning, generally, of its dissemination in India. *The Hindu* Magazine section for 19 October 2003 reported "Islamic English Schools" coming up in Mumbai. The sponsors of these schools envisage a radically different generation of Muslims: English-speaking, academically on par with the best, and thoroughly Islamic in conduct and appearance. *The Hindu* for the next day (20 October 2003) reported the activities of an NGO called LABS (Life Achievements Business Schools), which "selects students in the age group of 15–25, and gives them a three-month programme in spoken English. Students who have never studied in the English medium have developed sufficient competence to address huge gatherings confidently and in the last three to four years, 500 men and women of this level have been given jobs" (N. Vittal).

Yet another significant, if worrisome, trend in corporate India is the slow and steady marginalisation of regional languages.

The Indian middle class has increasingly spurned the languages of India by keeping its scions from regions and cultures from which they have sprung. An extremely mobile and freewheeling ethos and practice have trained middle-class children to adapt to pan-Indian "English" ways in terms of lifestyle and career options. A report from Mumbai, again, announces the recent decision of the Maharashtra State Board of Secondary and Higher Education to discontinue public examinations in Malayalam, Kannada, Bangla, Telugu, Tamil, Sindhi, Punjabi and Ardhamagadhi. Students who appear for the 2005 examinations will only have "Special English" instead, if they do not want to opt for the third language of the state, Marathi. There are finer nuances to this decision. The decision not to allow Bengali and Malayalee children to study their languages, for example, is unlikely to affect their respective languages because they are state-owned and sponsored, but a language like Sindhi has no state or official sponsorship. The Sindhi Forum is understandably angry at the Maharashtra Board's decision because their "5,000-year-old language" is part of their mental and emotional make-up, which travels and settles with them wherever the Sindhis go. The English of "corporate" India is dealing the hardest blow to languages like Sindhi, already fighting a losing battle against Hindi and English.

The Week magazine for November 9, 2003 ran a cover story on "Desi Craze for English", the language that opens a "world of opportunity" for young people in India. It also surveyed the government initiatives in at least three states – West Bengal, Rajasthan and Punjab – to bring back English at the primary level so that their wards do not suffer in national competition. *The Week* reports have come from virtually every corner of India: Patna, Pune, Srinagar, Hyderabad, Mumbai, Alibaug, Delhi, Himachal Pradesh and Kolkata. All tell us the same story of the demand and supply of English, the new product of corporate India. Watchers of this new India have also been reporting the vertiginous changes overtaking our social scene: business-as-usual under the aegis of English; lifestyle stores, and the mountains of commodities stocked therein; land and satellite communication packages; lifestyle foods and beverages, and the diseases that go with them; hasty marriages and leisurely repentance; single-parent families; latch-key kids; "instant" and easy entertainment in alienated cubby-holes; property bought on mortgages and credit cards; and an amazing personal mobility that makes young lives old in a matter of twenty years. Now all of this cannot be blamed on English, or English alone, but it is sure that the Indian social geography has changed, thanks to English-operated technologies. The cell phone and imaging services reach one, no matter what language one uses, only through English. And there is no decent product in today's India whose "literatures", or operating manuals, are available to a consumer in Indian languages.

English has created a pan-Indian brand-consciousness. It has become difficult to sell any product in the Indian market unless English endorses its brand. No wonder English itself is a brand Indians recognise and respect. A good example of this brand consciousness is the alliance of cricket and cola. Whether the game induced thirst, or the other way round, is debatable, but both together have endorsed the complete severance of Indian mind from the reality of our thirst. Both of course are "English" in origin, and if anyone in India doubted it, there is the language that underscores this fact and goes on to celebrate the "new" English that infuses a new vigour into the advertising lingo: *yeh dil maange more* and *life ho to aisi*. This is the best illustration of the role of English among Indian languages: the superb intensifier and catalyst of our modern linguistic imagination, and the instant integrative potential of English that an Indian language can readily exploit to its advantage.

ENGLISH AND THE INDIAN POSTMODERN

Many people living in parts of the world away from "home" sometimes feel that no home is too far or too near for anybody. In other words, the world seems to have suddenly shrunk in dimension. This may be due to the relentless work of electronic technology, mainly the SMS, TV and PC. Our nearest TV set preaches three to four religions in languages we seem to understand, relays programmes that target virtually all age groups and tastes. English has taught us that it is no great sin to learn another language, and through English we have entered domains hitherto barred to our knowledge – other foreign languages, cultures and sub-cultures of other ethnic groups, of other age and professional groups, interests or lifestyles. In short, the *otherness* of English, now subsumed in the otherness of cultures so unlike ours and that of English, has ceased to matter. In postmodern India, "packages" and "deals" from every part of the world have reached us mainly through English. We do not feel the "shock" anymore, the "shock" other cultures used to bring to the premodern homogeneous cultures of India.

The two great advantages English has had among Indian languages are:

1. Its amazing resilience and
2. Its great adaptability.

English is probably among the very few languages that have not only travelled so far and wide in the world, but one that has survived local resistance from other languages the world over. This has given it a remarkable resilience and adaptability which translate in many cultures into one's other language. A language in need is a language indeed.

* * *

After this introductory chapter on the history and social background of the *correspondence* between Indian English fiction and film, I have explored the idea of correspondence as similarities of themes between various texts of fiction and film (Chapter 2). There I have discussed some stock stories and standard motifs that are the hallmarks of both the genres. I have also described how fiction and film in Indian English self-reflexively refer to English, English literature and Indian English literature. This becomes important to show that the *correspondences* occur within an *autonomous* culture of English in India that is complete with internal cross-references.

Next follows an analysis of the dominant point of view – the social perspective – in these films and works of fiction. I have tried to demonstrate how the perception and presentation of society through English follows a set pattern. I have differentiated as well as compared the many varieties of this point of view across the sub-genres within fiction and film – the NRI films, diasporic fiction, parody films, etc. I argue here that there are social and cultural assumptions and beliefs that characterise the "English" Indians, and these get reflected in their fiction and films. For proper contextualisation I have added at appropriate places brief passages on the Indian English point of view as found in other media like newspaper, television, music videos, advertisements, websites, etc. This makes Chapter 3.

The correspondences are not limited to a mere similarity of themes and settings. In a subtle way the fiction in Indian English is getting modelled, consciously or unconsciously, after films. Contemporary Indian English fiction is narrated in a way that makes it resemble films. In Chapter 4, with specific references to a recent graphic novel, I have listed some of the most common cultural stereotypes of English fiction and films in India. These are also stereotypes of the Indian English culture and its visual culture. I argue that photographs and cartoons are used to evoke programmed responses in many Indian English textual contexts.

The concluding part, Chapter 5, stresses the responses the two genres have made and continue making to the social matrix, and also how the social life of English responds back, making it a *correspondence* in the full sense. The conclusion also briefly recapitulates the other correspondences explained earlier.

This book has not discussed in detail some of the Indian English films like *Bride and Prejudice, Morning Raga, Sins, White Noise, 15 Park Avenue* and *Being Cyrus*. My attempt has been to identify the general trend, and not record the phenomenon comprehensively. Some of the important Indian English films are mentioned only in passing (Revathi's *Mitr*, for example) because one or more films of their type is discussed in detail. Another omission is the film *English, August*. The novel is however an important text for my study. This leaves no room for the confusion whether this book is about Indian English fiction-into-film, which it clearly is not.

Indian fiction in English today is too vast an area to be covered in one time. I have studied here a novel each or a short story that is representative of the sub-genre to which it belongs. Hence, Shobha De from popular fiction, Salman Rushdie and Jhumpa Lahiri to represent NRI fiction, Shashi Tharoor and Upamanyu Chatterjee from "Indian" Indian English fiction, and Sarnath Banerjee from the new generation.

NOTES

1. The same cross-section of urban youth were the avid readers of "pulp" fiction in cheap paperbacks.
2. Like in Hitchcock's *Vertigo*, a character feels he is being pushed down a height by invisible hands. See Ray, Satyajit. "Ratanbabu and That Man". *Stories*. Calcutta: Seagull, 1987. 63–78.
3. Narayan was displeased with the gratuitous flamboyance with which the film was made. It departed too far from the original, and Narayan

complained about not being able to see his Malgudi in the panoramic locations of Jaipur, where the producer Dev Anand shot the film. For Narayan's account of the film, see his *My Days: A Memoir*. Delhi: Orient Paperbacks, 1986. 171–174.

4. All leaving English, and some Hindi and other Indian language channels, found it eminently newsworthy to report as a "top story" the fact that 1,25,000 young people sat the CAT examinations throughout the country in November 2004. All top corporate managing-job aspirants, the CAT examinees, consider "English" to be as demanding a component of the CAT paper as "Quantitative Analysis" and "Mathematics". To the very select respondents, who were featured on these channels, "This year's English was much easier than the earlier years'." Of course the whole CAT exercise is administered in English.

CHAPTER 2

The Stories of English India

INDIAN English fiction and Indian English films began to show clear signs of correspondence in the 1980s. This was when Indian English film became a distinct genre departing from the tradition of co-productions of the Merchant–Ivory kind. The stories of films and prose fiction of this time are situated in the middle-class suburbs of metropolitan India. The middle class of urban India was fast preparing in those days to welcome the tide of globalisation that was to set in in the 1990s. Economic reforms and social changes followed. The face of the metros and small towns all over the country changed. The role English played in this transformation – how it was instrumental in the cultural changes, English's emergence as a way of life – can be seen from the English fiction and films from that period up to now. Many of them are representative and emblematic of the culture that English created.

As we have seen in the first chapter, there was a major shift in the Indian English literary scene in the 1980s. The themes of rural and small-town India, found in the novels of R. K. Narayan, Raja Rao and Mulk Raj Anand, now got replaced on a wholesale basis with city-oriented stories set in the metros. English fiction in India became more or less preoccupied with the English lifestyles of urban India. The new genre, Indian English films, followed the same representational style. The preference of Indians for English becomes a theme in the earliest Indian English film itself. *36 Chowringhee Lane* features two important characters, Samresh and Nandita, who typify the educated elite of Calcutta that relishes western ways of culture.

It shows Indians gaining "Englishness" by association with the English, their literature, music and many other cultural products. Violet Stoneham, the lead figure in the film, is an Anglo-Indian who has chosen to live in India after its independence. An English teacher by profession, she specialises in Shakespeare.[1] Her solitary apartment, furnished the way the colonial houses usually are, instantly catches Samresh's Anglophile fancy, and he requests her permission to use it. As an aspiring writer – presumably in English, since he refers to himself as a "James Joyce in the making" – Samresh somehow feels this house should better inspire his imaginative flights. That an Indian writer should fancy himself to be in the same league as a canonical English author and be inspired by the British ambience of an apartment is evidence of the "English" imagination that still drives Indian English writing. Despite being a proud Bengali, Samresh prefers to inherit, and does inherit, the English literary tradition when he might well have sought a place for himself in Bangla literature.

The obsession with everything English, however, is not confined merely *within* the film *36 Chowringhee Lane*. It spills over the text in interesting ways to its levels of reception. The references to Shakespeare are examples for this. In the last scene of the film, Violet Stoneham recites a long passage from *King Lear* – "Come, let's away to prison . . ." – which, from her own, and the cinematic point of view, aptly expresses the pathos of the neglected old woman's condition. But the filmmaker expects the audience to empathise with the woman chiefly through this specific passage in *King Lear*. The question is: How justified is Aparna Sen in taking for granted a fair familiarity with Shakespeare among the Indian audience for her film? There is little surprise in the occurrence of a Shakespeare quote in an Indian English film, given the fact that its audience are mainly the English-educated Indians, and the subject English in the Indian curriculum is still *British* literature for all intents and purposes. The larger and more intriguing question is: Would our audience not see old-age miseries as such in India without recourse to the Shakespeare of England and the king Lear of yore?

Aparna Sen's movie is still full of fictional, yet accurate, accounts of the defining traits of Anglophone India. With a taste for vintage English popular music, Samaresh manages to snatch the gramophone record collection ofViolet as a wedding gift from her. Later, even as the Samresh–Nandita couple snubs the old lady, they are seen to be swaying with friends to the music from the lady's collection. The whole gathering at the party, all in western dress, seems to recognise and enjoy such songs as "lipstick on your collar . . ." and "red polka dot bikini . . .". Signs are also to be found in these sequences of an emerging new morality adapted from the European, to suit the Indian context. In the classroom where Ms Stoneham delivers Shakespearian dialogues, teenage students are reading comic books under the desk. A boy and a girl are silently discussing a steamy kiss depicted in the comic. This peripheral scene, which highlights the pathetic condition of the lady, is significantly true to a generation, which, with a will to emulation, eagerly imbibes what English brings to them. Representative of the same generation are Samresh and Nandita, who entertain no scruples about premarital sex. But they still talk in Bangla to each other and do not renounce any benefits of belonging to the "babu" segment of Calcutta. This indicates beyond doubt that the cultural mutation of a certain generation into western ways was by no means total, but a selective integration resulting in the *Indian English sub-culture.*

THE GENERATION GAP

A common theme in many of the Indian English films, novels and stories is the tension between two generations – usually the old pitted against the new. "The generations at odds" has almost become a stock problematic in the two forms. But here, one should do more than confuse it with the conflict universally thought to exist between all preceding and succeeding generations because in this case a particular stance with respect to the changing face of the society is involved. Here the later the generation, the more inclined it is towards the culture imported via English. Contrary to what we normally expect, the rift between the quarrelling generations is, in reality, as negligible as it is seemingly serious because the older people in the films and stories/novels studied here are ultimately supportive of the new path their successors have chosen. As some of the following examples would show, the conservative old folk eventually give their tacit consent to the new, realising the benefits English has to offer, and seeing English only as the latest in the same tradition in which they have also been raised.

In Shobha De's *Socialite Evenings*, the main character Karuna exemplifies the rebellious youth of the urban India. In the face of her parents' threats, she eats meat at school and later takes up modelling as a profession, to which her father responds thus: "Do you mean to disgrace us completely? This is not something girls of respectable families do" and "Disgraceful! Cheap! Filthy! No Brahmin girl has ever stooped so low" (24). About the education the girls receive within the family, the narrator Karuna says:

> The one commodity that was never short in supply in our house was reading material. We subscribed to several magazines including the pricey *National Geographic*. Plus, Father had carefully maintained his own highly priced collection of classics. We sisters had access to Dickens, Jane Austen, Shaw and Shakespeare, Nehru and Radhakrishnan. Also, Father had a remarkable memory for literature – he could quote from Twain, Shakespeare and Bhagavat Gita. Interestingly, in this I'm probably unique,

> though I am glad to say it lasted only till I grew to adulthood, I'm perhaps the only person who graduated from the classics via cult books like *The Fountainhead* (for a long time I was determined to marry a man like Howard Roark and even I had a tremendous crush on an architect in the neighbourhood though it is highly unlikely he even noticed me) to outright trash. (16)

The father in this novel is part of a generation that had had its equal share of both modernity and native culture. He belongs to the earlier breed of Anglophone Indians who successfully straddle between Indian culture and the new ideas brought by western education. As a type this parent figure can be seen in a range of fiction and films in Indian English. In Upamanyu Chatterjee's *English, August*, Agastya Sen's father, the Governor, is a person who reads *Reader's Digest*, Marcus Aurelius and *Katha Upanishad* (169, 172). The grandmother quoting Shakespeare in *Bollywood/Hollywood*, the bride's parents Mr and Mrs Verma in *Monsoon Wedding*, the characters played by Anupam Kher and Shaheen Khan in *Bend It Like Beckham* are all-ambivalent towards the new reality. In contrast, their children invariably flout the mores that bind them and become a more carefree and relaxed people.

Bollywood/Hollywood is the best example of the very evident compromise with the well-guarded tradition by the young. It appears that the whole family shown in the movie stands for the preservation of "Indian culture". The hero Rahul's rich father[2] dies giving his son these words of wisdom from his deathbed: "Remember Rahul, sacrifice is the brightest torch of Indian family values. Just like the opening of the Olympics, Rahul, run, run with the torch until you light the big torch." Later, the priggish grandmother nearly aborts Rahul's proposed marriage with his white girlfriend, who happens to be a pop star, and who in turn dies while shooting in Hollywood. On her meeting with Rahul's family, the grandmother asks the girlfriend questions like, "Which caste are you?", "Which village are you [from]?" and "Will you become a Hindu?" before finally dismissing her as a "white whore". The family is devoutly Hindu and Indian with poojas and bhajans happening at the home and a large *Aum* in the Devanagari displayed at the illuminated gate of the mansion. Sue is an Indian, but is presumed to be Hispanic. Rahul contracts her to act as his new Indian girlfriend. Her real name is Sunita Singh. As soon as the fastidious old woman begins to like Sue, she mellows down and shelves her standards. She winks at the fact that Sue is not a vegetarian and that she attends parties. It transpires that the grandmother after all was no less liberal than the boys and girls, before she donned the role of the incorrigible matriarch. This is in fact only expected of a lady who is very fluent in English and quotes Shakespeare every now and then.

Similarly, in *Bend It Like Beckham*, Jesminder's father (Anupam Kher) allows her to join the football team touring America despite it being the day of her sister's marriage. Neither of the parents initially wants her to make football a career – "What family would want a daughter-in-law who can run around kicking football but can't make round chapattis?" But it is not the communal instincts of their being Sikh or the fear of excommunication from the community that finally prevails in resolving Jesminder's woes, but the ambitious prospect of her being an international footballer beyond all ethnic identity barriers. The choice between the prospects of ending up as yet another meek Punjabi bride in Britain and that of becoming a football celebrity is that between conventional and liberal ways of life. *Bend It Like Beckham* – and Indian English films in general – is fervently for the latter option, as the quotation in the advertisement for this film testifies: "Who wants to cook alu-gobi when you can bend the ball like Beckham?"

The new generation developed a liberal attitude as they grew up. Sociologically it paralleled a certain devolution of English language. The earlier generation had found it a good medium for intellectual imports and serious discourse. It, therefore, valued the "high culture" that accompanied English – perhaps as the Sanskrit of the modern times. This explains the taste of the father in *Socialite Evenings* for Twain, Dickens, Shakespeare and Nehru. Again, Meenaxi's father-in-law in *Mr and Mrs Iyer* is an endocrinologist who strictly adheres to the caste system. People of this kind kept English to special circles and topics, not letting it influence and "contaminate" traditional culture. But the modern means of communication and easy methods of dissemination have made English more ubiquitous and rendered it a part of everyday life. English in India underwent a transition from an intellectual language to one of conversation and of "popular culture" of a certain kind. Most of the Indian English films and "pulp fiction" by writers like Shobha De have contributed much to the making of this English "popular culture". These writers' themes refer back to this sub-culture of English in many ways. Karuna of *Socialite Evenings* had "graduated" from classics to cult books – to be inspired in life only by the latter. If we take this example literally, the sharp turn in the preferences of the new generation will be clear.

Like a common pattern, an unprecedented set of values, moral liberties and attitudes have come to characterise the young people of the fictional world of Indian English fiction and films. Replacing an Indian language, English has taken over (or is gradually taking over) the task of making many minds function. Hence the prevalence of ideas, thoughts and lifestyle that are, like properties, untranslatably inherent in the new language. It can be claimed that the most attractive and sought-after ways of city life today come in the company of English.

THE SELF-REFLEXIVITY OF ENGLISH IN FICTION AND FILMS

Some works of fiction and film in Indian English seem self-conscious about their medium. They often make an explicit reference to the use of English in India and to things that are generally understood in the context of the English sub-culture. For example, in Dev Benegal's *Split Wide Open*, the character K. P., an orphan in a Bombay slum, is shown to speak fluent English. The explanation for this is his upbringing. Father Bruno, the missionary who runs the orphanage where K. P. was brought up, had taught him English, because the Father knew English meant "the keys to the kingdom". The film shows street children learning English from the Father because they realise that "if you know English you don't have to work hard". Significantly, the film was written by an established Indian English writer Upamanyu Chatterjee. Chatterjee's detailed differentiation between the advanced English-speaking India and the old underdeveloped India in his famed novel *English, August* reads like a thesis on the contemporary scene of English in India. There are numerous references here not only to English and English literature, but also to Indian English literature. The perspective of the narrator, the protagonist, as well as of the whole novel as such, is that of metropolitan English India – all the major characters are bureaucrats and government officials. An IAS officer Srivastav speaks about the instrumentality of English:

> "In Azamganj, where I come from, I studied in a Hindi-medium school. Now people with no experience of these schools say that that's a good thing, because we should throw English out of India. Rubbish, I say, many other things are far more important. I *know* bhai. There is not a single good teacher in these schools in these smaller places. How can there be, when their working conditions are so bad, when they themselves pass out of such schools and colleges? When I went to college in Lucknow,

I felt completely stupid. So I began to read English on my own. I had to, because English was compulsory for the Civil Services exam. So I read Shakespeare and Wordsworth and people like that, very difficult. *It is still important to know English, it gives one*" he fisted his hand, "*confidence*". [Italics in the original] (59–60)

Some characters in *English, August* are readers of English books – the IAS officer Menon has read Ruth Prawer Jhabvala's *Heat and Dust* (39); Govind Sathe, the journalist, carries a copy of the book of the BBC TV serial *Yes Minister* (42); and Agastya Sen himself reads the *Gita* and *Ramayana* in English. Having made a cartoon about Indian English writers, Sathe makes the following comment:

"I wanted to suggest an Indian writer writing about India, after having spent many years abroad, or living there. There are hundreds of them – well, if not hundreds, at least twenty-five. I find these people absurd, full with one mixed-up culture and writing about another, what kind of audience are they aiming at? That's why their India is just not real, a place of fantasy, or of confused metaphysics, a subcontinent of goons. All their Indians are caricatures. Why is that? Because there really are no universal stories, because each language is an entire culture." (47–48)

Govind Sathe here makes an accurate observation about the Indian English literature of one era, and unconsciously vindicates the kind of English writing in which he himself figures as a character. The context, the language, the speaker and the nature of this statement amply disprove the content of it. Characters of his kind become possible precisely because "each language is an entire culture", and that language which is Sathe's culture is Indian English. This passage in *English, August* can be considered the disguised self-validation of Indian English literature and culture, which endorse themselves while seemingly continuing to believe in the "otherness" of English. The company that engages in this conversation is a group of typical English Indians. When they come together, the language of the group is invariably English. Their conversation will usually include generalised observations as in the example cited above. Today there is a great probability of encountering similar groups in trains, clubs, restaurants, airports, and public places in general. This is the hard evidence for the actual existence of the Indian English culture in our society.

One broad understanding of a language is as a culture, as an autonomous collection of traditions. Many of its specific constituents like allusions and specialised references may retain no meaning outside the traditions that a particular language includes. For English, the potential range of references is overwhelmingly large and international. To know English would be to expand one's potential access to an unlimited range of international subjects, the mention of which in regionally located languages might seem out of context. Both Indian English fiction and Indian English film abound in references to many such internationally shared themes of life. For example, in Rushdie's fiction the events are set partly in India and partly abroad. *The Moor's Last Sigh* is set in Kerala, Bombay and Spain. A novel that demands from the reader a knowledge about the moors of Granada, the Jews of Mattanchery and the far-right politics of Bombay, is certainly presupposing an international sensibility, which in India roughly equals a sound knowledge of English and tastes and interests acquired through English. This means that a work of Indian English fiction delimits its readership by virtue of its choice of subjects. The themes of *The Moor's Last Sigh* are national events like the Bhopal gas tragedy and the Bombay riots. It is undeniable that English must inform a consciousness that can connect all the above themes into coherence.

Removed from the high intellectual content of a Rushdiean novel, the Indian English films too contain innumerable instances where an international or "English" topic is spontaneously invoked. The film *Let's Talk* (director: Ram Madhvani) opens with showing the texts of the letters Nikhil and Radhika, husband and wife, write to each other. Although very personal and intimate, this correspondence is in English. In one of the letters, Nikhil sends a poem by T. S. Eliot, "A Dedication to My Wife", and the line "of lovers whose bodies smell of each other" is highlighted on the screen. In *Socialite Evenings*, the narrator describes a lover of hers:

> He was also a handy reference library. I respected his scholarship and his literary passions. "Let's go then, you and I, while the evening stretches across the sky," he'd say by way of an invitation he knew I wouldn't take up. (I didn't recognise the poem either!) He would recommend books, stray bits of poetry, an article in the *New Yorker*, a film he'd enjoyed. I discovered Yeats and Kurosawa, Yevteshenko and Maria Callas. (70–71)

Furthermore, the names that occur in the narration and the characters' conversation include the Beatles, Ayn Rand (82), Humphrey Bogart (69), Marlon Brando (129), Barbara Cartland (132), Liz Taylor (133), Sherlock Holmes and *Gone with the Wind* (150). The section of the society which these films and books depict and for which they depict it have a fair knowledge about Eliot, Holmes and Hollywood – it is almost as if these are part of the Indian English general knowledge. The citation of Shakespeare and Joyce in *36 Chowringheee Lane* may be remembered here. The all importance of David Beckham's image in *Bend It Like Beckham*, catering to the audiences' eagerness to buy the glamour and myth that surrounds this British player, proves the same point. There exists an enthusiastic acceptance of things international among the receptors of these products. Raja Choudhary in *Mr and Mrs Iyer* mentions to his companion Meenaxi that Madonna wears bindi as a fashion. But a person like Meenaxi, too orthodox to show any interest in figures like Madonna, corrects him, saying, "She [Madonna] used to [wear bindis.]" Such unexpected behaviour in spite of traditional beliefs, is common among people whose education has made them part of a public world they share with others. In *Everybody Says I'm Fine*, the failed film star Rage decides to commit suicide. But he immediately wishes he were famous like Ernest Hemingway when he took his own life – one of the most ambitious deaths one can ask for. In *Bollywood/Hollywood*, Rahul recites a poem by Pablo Neruda to woo Sunita, and the same film uses subtitle equivalents of a footnote to explain a reference to the old Hindi film *Devdas*. The supposition here is that the intended viewer is familiar with Neruda but not with a once-popular Hindi film.

To cite another example from fiction, Saladin Chamcha, a confirmed Anglophile in Rushdie's *The Satanic Verses*, is dismayed at the rootedness and confinement of life in India. He longs for the great cities of the world:

> Salahuddin Chamchawala had understood by his thirteenth year that he was destined for that cool Vilayet full of crisp promises of pound sterling at which the magic bill fold had hinted, and he grew increasingly impatient of that Bombay of dust, vulgarity, policemen in shorts, transvestites, movie fanzines, pavement sleepers and the rumoured singing whores of the Grant Road . . . He was fed up of textile factories and local trains and all the confusion and superabundance of the place, and dreamed for that dream-Vilayet of poise and moderation that had come to obsess him by night and day. His favourite playground rhymes were those that yearned for foreign cities: kitchy-con-kitchy ki-kitchy-con stanty- eye kitchy- ople kitchy- cople kitchy- con-stanti-nople. And his favourite game was the version of grandmother's footsteps in which, when he was *it*, he would turn his back on upcreeping playmates to gabble out, like a mantra, like a spell, the six letters of his dream-city, *ellowen deeowen*. In his secret heart, he crept silently upon London, letter by letter, just as his friends crept up to him. *Ellowen deeowen*. (37)

Finally, we have Mira Nair's *Monsoon Wedding*, where the fatherless girl Ria (Shefali Shetty) wants to attend a creative writing programme in America. The family is worried about the financial part of her ambition, but nevertheless welcomes it. They realise that nowadays there is a lot of money in writing and specifically discuss a certain Indian lady having recently won the Booker Prize. The mention of Arundhati Roy in this context is very significant. The impulsive association of creative writing with creative writing in English reveals a feature of consciousness of a section of the society for whom to write literature means to write in English and join the Indian English club. The similarities of allusions and a common cultural field as source of inspirations for the texts (fictions and film) underscore the *autonomy* of the English sub-culture in India, which produces for itself its own fiction and films in a strong inevitable correspondence.

NOTES

1. It is intriguing that it is mostly an *English* classroom that an Indian film will take the audience to, when it has to show a classroom. This trend derives from the unconscious synonymy in the Indian psyche between education and English. While in *36 Chowringhee Lane* it may not have been accidental, most Indian language films have time and again conformed to this stereotype of a classroom.
2. The father is addressed as "Daddyji", a new amalgamation of the informality and endearment in the English word "daddy" with the formal and honorific suffix *ji* from Hindi. It is a highly illustrative sample of the result of English's long cohabitation with Indian culture and languages.

CHAPTER 3

The Degree of Anglicisation and the External Point of View

INDIAN English fiction and Indian English films show people whose primary language of social and private interaction is mainly English. They consistently show us the attitudes, behaviour and locales characteristic of this community.[1] But they also show people who do not know or speak English, and who serve as foils to the English-speaking protagonists. The way these films and fiction portray non-English-speaking and less-English-speaking characters can tell us about the social status of English with respect to other languages.

If we study closely some sample situations from Indian English fiction and films, it would make clear the difference between using English and using an Indian language in a social situation. We would be able to see an "Indian English point of view" that all presentations of such situations have in common. This is also the social point of view from which most of these films and fiction are narrated. We find two broad categories of characters in terms of the English they can command: one, the English-speaking urban Indians, who are the protagonists of these stories; two, the ones who are less fluent or not fluent at all in English, and who play the peripheral and supporting roles in the stories. The latter are often the subjects of mild ridicule because of their "unmodern" ways. The formula of comedy used in these works is the key to the sensibility of the class of English speakers who appreciate them. The common butts of ridicule in these fictions and films are the non-English-speaking or the less-English-speaking characters.

In the film *Monsoon Wedding* the character played by Kulbhushan Kharbandha has semi-comic attributes. As the whole family speaks English, he speaks Punjabi. Unlike the other NRI members of the family, he is employed in the Middle East (Muscat), while others are from the major English-speaking countries – the USA, Australia, etc. In one scene where he is shown alone, this middle-aged man is seen to be combing his hair in front of the mirror humming a romantic Hindi song, "*kaho na pyaar hai . . .*". The little girl Alia enters carrying a book and asks him the meaning of a word she had chanced upon in the book she has been reading. The word is "uxorious", and he obviously does not know the meaning. He struggles to conceal his ignorance and decides it is surely a misspelling. The word, according to him, should have been "luxurious". The serious part of this funny episode is the social aspect of it. The scriptwriter, the director and the audience, who are confident of their English, are slyly and collectively having fun at the ignorant Kulbhushan Kharbandha, whose English is poor.

The contrast between the non-English characters and the protagonists is a device in these films that helps emphasise the more "refined" culture of the latter. The ridiculous foils help us see the heroes in better definition. To take another example, the film director Subrahmanyam is a laughing stock in Nagesh Kukunoor's farce *Bollywood Calling*. A director of popular Hindi movies, Subrahmanyam embodies the stereotype of the "unmannered" and "crude" Indian. This style of making caricatures of people like Subrahmanyam, or the "native type", is an instance of what we can call the "external point of view". It is equal to taking an external and apparently detached stand and laughing at presumed inferiors. From this privileged point of view, the supposed "uncivilised" aspects of India are mocked at in writing, films, cartoons and media in general.

Subrahmanyam's English, with its marked regional accent,

his non-westernised (and exaggerated) manners, lack of punctuality and disorganised ways make us laugh. He stands in contrast with the American hero Pat's polished manners and systematic work culture. The film is evidently taking sides with people like Pat, whom English has made "refined", and their laughter at Subrahmanyam is fully justified.[2] It is important to notice the social bearings of the smugness that makes comedy of this kind possible. The culture of English in India has consistently had this extra confidence in itself as part of its mindset. The comic effect is born from the consensus within this culture about what is inferior. Hence the construction of incompetence in English as most undesirable, unfortunate and laughable.

One often sees English-literate Indian sensibility finding fault with the "native" behaviour. The irritable brother and sister travelling in the bus in *Mr and Mrs Iyer* are an example. Because they are unsociable, the brother and sister have to be, by default, speaking an Indian language, and cannot be shown as speakers of English. Thus, according to the unconscious rules of representation in the Indian English films, they speak Hindi. The same rules work in *American Desi* where the Punjabi-speaking roommate of the protagonist is a comic figure. His Punjabi and excessive nostalgia for things Indian are his comic traits.

In a film like *Mumbai Matinee*, the segregation of characters according to their languages into serious and non-serious ones makes for a good study of the cultural attributes of English and other languages. As usual, the comic figures are shown to speak Hindi. The "baba", his secretary, the film producer, the aspiring actor who accompanies the producer, and the Bengali police inspector are featured in light situations, each one of them behaving eccentrically. Interestingly, the songs of this film are in Hindi. The Indian English film cannot probably do justice to the convention of song in Indian cinema if it starts to have songs in English. This leaves us wondering if the Indian English film is not a chip off the old Bollywood block.

It is interesting that in none of the Indian English works, fiction or film, can we quickly discern an absolute condemnation of Indian languages and culture. Conversely, their attitude is apparently one of respect to the "traditions" of India. All the protagonists, despite being speakers of English, are at heart "lovers" of their mother tongue and native culture. It is just that English gives their personality and outlook an added edge over the less-privileged fellow countrymen. In *Mumbai Matinee*, the soliloquies of the hero Debu Chatterjee are in Hindi. Also, in matters of religion or the sacred, an Indian language is always used.[3] The Punjabi marriage ceremonies, the folksongs that precede them, but are sung in a modern metropolitan household (*Monsoon Wedding*), far removed from the folk culture where they originated, are all evidence of the new cultural amalgamation. In fact, the serious characters' use of their mother tongue is extolled as an act of enlightened respect for tradition. But the other section, the non-English-literate characters, uses Indian languages because they have no English. In the world of Indian English films, even to speak an Indian language respectably and with true belonging, one has to first know English, lest one should be excluded from the "dignified" English-class. Anglicisation, in sum, seems to be a measure of respectability in the Indian English world. The more steeped one is in English – meaning not just the language, but a way of life – the greater one's chances are of being considered rational, sensible, well mannered, sociable and educated.

English has reinterpreted and re-presented our reality to ourselves. The ways of seeing, understanding, determining and judging the world are heavily dependent on the language that inevitably accompanies these processes. This explains why thinking in English about India gives a picture of India that is different from the India described in an Indian language. English seems to bring in a neutrality of tone to a discussion because of its apparent un-rootedness in terms of a specific geography in India. But this neutrality has often turned into a disengaged perspective that views India with a putatively uninfluenced external "objective" eye. Through rampant, and often mindless, repetition in literature, film, newspapers, cartoons, television programmes, public speeches, lectures, university classrooms and discussion forums, this perspective has firmly embedded itself in the minds of the Indian whose only medium of accessing information and knowledge about his/her India is English. We can attempt to describe the different levels and degrees at which the external point of view operates. Its nature and function will become more evident as we proceed from one example to another of writing and films in Indian English.

The characteristic perspective of Indian English discourses has mainly two distinct forms. The first one relates to that component of these discourses which originates from, is located in, and mainly circulates, not in India, but in various parts of the English-speaking world outside India. This perspective is usually prevalent among the NRIs. It comprises the impressions, ideas, nostalgic memories, anecdotes and hopes about India. Images of this are easily illustrated by consulting popular magazine pictures, the kitsch of calendar art, music albums, and perhaps a whole lot of tourist manuals and guides that represent India in magic splendour. *Since* a considerable number of Indian English films and stories stem from an NRI basis, their common point of view deserves closer study. The following section "India Abroad" talks about the specific texts that project India as Indians and others from outside see it.

If the first kind of Indian English perspective is that of the Indians living outside under actual expatriation, the second belongs to those who are at what we can figuratively call different stages of virtual and progressive expatriation. This second attitude is the result of *assuming* – in the double sense of thinking, imagining, as well as taking power – a notionally "higher" status, power and sensibility over the non-Anglophone India. This is the second way English shapes the picture of India through various discursive forms. This mode of thinking is so prevalent and taken for granted today that its very ubiquity makes it almost invisible to the analytic eye. The section "The External Point of View" traces that multi-modal perspective so frequent in the English-aided streams of contemporary Indian culture.

INDIA ABROAD

Critics and readers have divided the contemporary Indian English fiction into two – English fiction written in India and that written by Indians living abroad. Indian English writing as one whole phenomenon is the cumulative result of literary input from various sources irrespective of the location of the contributors. To be classed among Indian English literature, any work should satisfy only one free condition: it should possess some measure of "Indian experience". Hence, writers of such various nationalities and backgrounds as V. S. Naipaul, Shashi Tharoor, Jhumpa Lahiri, Salman Rushdie, Manjula Padmanabhan, Vikram Seth, Bharati Mukherjee, Arundhati Roy and Ruth Prawer Jhabvala become "Indian writers in English". Many of the themes and stories are therefore not located in India at all, but are about Indians living abroad. Based on where the theme is set, it is easy to make the distinction between the fiction of India and the diasporic fiction. The distinction is easily extensible to the body of Indian English films too. Almost half of the Indian English films are either made abroad or target an international audience.

In the 1980s and 90s, English literature by Indians became immensely popular all over the world. From the 1990s onwards Indian English films also began to enjoy the same popularity among expatriate Indian and other audiences abroad. With the aid of the English language, fiction and films from India have not only become successful themselves, but also popularised abroad the idea of India. This idea of India, narrated through many similar novels, stories and films, has come to obey a particular pattern and have a set perspective. This perspective is evidently due to the internationalism of outlook shared by the communities these stories and films depict. In a foreign land, speaking English, the Indians abroad look at India in various interesting ways that define their ideas about nationality, belonging, identity, culture and tradition. The NRI way of imagining India (through English) can be illustrated with examples from a few samples of diasporic Indian literature and films.

The reason to call the expatriates' perception of India a disengaged picture is that it is derived mostly not from lived experience but textual presentations. This includes printed matter like books and maps, visual matter as cinema and television, and the mixed medium of the internet. In all the stories and films analysed in this section, we can see the NRIs constantly resorting to Hindi movies to feel culturally closer to home (the roommate in *American Desi*, the family watching an Amitabh Bachan film in *Bend It Like Beckham*, the Punjabi father in *Bollywood/Hollywood*, etc). The second reason for the dissociation of the global Indians' perspective from the real India lies in the cultural confusion of the second generation Indians, who are known as the "American Born Confused Desis". This phrase is the name of an "NRI" Indian English film. The stories and films represent two contradicting mentalities in them – a love for Indian tradition on the one hand, and on the other, a deliberate disowning of ethnic identities. Ironically, both the attitudes are part of the same external perspective about India. The understanding of India is usually no more deep than a knowledge of Indian food, a smattering of Hinduism, some Indian music and Indian dress. These are also the signs through which the expatriates preserve their "Indianness". In a story "This Blessed House" by Jhumpa Lahiri, it is the sari and salwar-kameez that women wear, and the samosas, that introduce an Indian ambience to a party thrown by the Sanjeev–Twinkle couple (151–2). In all other respects, lifestyle, outlook, they are more American than Indian.

In "A Temporary Matter" we see an Indian academic in an American university, Shukumar, doing research on agrarian revolts in India. His wife Shoba is a proof-reader. India comes to them in the form of Shoba's mother, who is a religious woman. Although the mother sets up a shrine and does pooja in the house, to the couple it is merely the "framed picture of a lavender-faced goddess" (9). To them India is a remote past symbolising underdevelopment. It is a power shutdown in the locality that reminds them of India:

> "It is like India," Shoba said, watching him tend his makeshift candelabra. "Sometimes the current disappears for hours at a stretch. I once had to attend an entire rice ceremony in the dark. The baby just cried and cried. It must have been so hot." (11)

A very superficial understanding, or sheer ignorance, about India is what many young people of Indian origin possess. India is something that has been put behind and is past even though it is the source of cultural and racial identity. The integration of these communities into the English-speaking mainstream has made the Indians' perception of India identical to the mainstream understanding. This can be explained in terms of the register of internationalism that naturally inheres in the English language and culture these diasporic communities live in. Here is an example from Bhararti Mukherjee's story "Hindus" for the vague telescopic notion of India common among Indians abroad:

It bothered Derek that I knew so little about my heritage. Islam is nothing more than a marauder's faith to me, but the Mogul emperors stayed a long time in the green delta of the Ganges, flattening and reflattening a fort in the village where I was born, and forcing my priestly ancestors to prove themselves brave. (129)

The narrator Leela had migrated to America and married an American called Derek. In the new society she manages to erase her previous identities, and markers such as caste now become for her matters of jest to be laughed away in the following casual and dismissive way:

I was a Bengali Brahmin: maharajas – not to put too sharp a point on it – were frankly beneath me, by at least one caste, though some of them, like Pat, would dispute it. Before my marriage to Derek, no one in my family, since our initial eruption from Vishnu's knee, had broken caste etiquette. (133)

In this story, an American uses the word "Hindi" to mean "Hindu", and Leela does not bother to correct it. Her explanation for this indifference can explain for us the very nature of many an Indian community abroad and their perception of India. In Leela's words:

I was about to correct her silly mistake – I'd learned from Derek to be easily incensed over ignorant confusions between Hindi and Hindus – but then I thought, why bother? Maybe she is right. That slight undetected error, call it an accent, isn't part of language at all. I speak Hindu. No matter what language I speak, it will come out slightly foreign, no matter how perfectly I mouth it. There is a whole world of us now. Speaking Hindu. (140)

Cinema, being a popular genre, lacks the subtlety and complexity of themes that fiction possesses. Therefore, in the NRI Indian English films, the signs that reveal the external, disengaged point of view about India are often obvious and easy to identify. In Piyush Dinkar Pandya's *American Desi*, the chief character is a university student called Krishnagopal Reddy. But he insists on calling himself "Kris", and resents that he was allotted a hostel room with three other Indians. The elaborate poojas his mother does when Kris leaves for the university, he dismisses as "religious crap". The film is full of stereotypes about India: an Indian teaching assistant always coming late to the class, and comments like "He is probably running on Indian standard time." Gowtam Rao, the teaching assistant, is fat and rotund. He wears a scarf around his neck and speaks English with an Indian accent. He causes a wave of laughter in the class by mispronouncing students' names during roll call and makes himself a laughing stock. Gautam brings a tiffin carrier to the canteen, washes his hands into it and wipes his mouth on the shirtsleeves – acts that are "typically Indian". At a bookstore, the Indian roommate picks up a copy of the *Kama Sutra* and flaunts it – an act the filmmaker feels would emphasise "Indianness", while he is simply repeating the stereotypical association of India and the *Kama Sutra.*

Nagesh Kukunoor's *Hyderabad Blues* gives a good example for the estranged Indian's way of perceiving India. Coming home from America after twelve years, the character Varun's idea of the home country has completely changed. He keeps cribbing about India – he has had to travel by train because of a pilot stir (India is a place where always people strike work). Travelling back home in a car, he exclaims: "Damn, I can't recognise this place anymore. My memory is poor. I am scared as any traveller is in a foreign land." Varun's sensibility has also succumbed to the external perspective. He reacts after watching *Hum Apke Hai Kaun?*: "Horrible movie dad, thirteen songs. No one needed an excuse to burst into a song." Later he has a debate with his girlfriend Aswini, who accuses him of being a deserter, to which he responds: "Is that what I am? Just because I had the good fortune to compare the two cultures, to take the best of both, and make my own? Well, I am part American."

THE EYE OF THE REAL OUTSIDER

While writing and filming India in English, directors and authors have often thought it more appropriate to tell their stories from a truly and genuinely "English" point of view. To achieve this, they have time and again included a native speaker in a main role, so that the predominant point of view does not clash with, but matches, the linguistic identity of the protagonist. Even the Indian protagonists will be practically European/ English in their outlook. This is an easy way to evade the painstaking task of working out a point of view in English that is completely Indian but pliably adapted to the English language. The idea of a "genuine" English-speaking character may also have been suggested by the awkward translational nature of the thoughts and speech of Indian characters in an English-medium textual existence. This seems to be the simple logic behind the prominent presence of non-Indians in Indian English films and fiction. It will be interesting to examine how these works co-opt an outsider and narrate an Indian story in a quasi-borrowed voice.

The earliest of Indian English films, *36 Chowringhee Lane*, has an Anglo-Indian in the central role. The film demands that the viewers' sympathies be with Violet Stoneham rather than with the Indian characters Samresh and Nandita. The film often breaks the objective point of view and drifts into the interior monologue of Violet – the best example would be the final scene where she recites Shakespeare to condole her own abandonment by the world. While making the film an English perspective must have come as infinitely handy to Aparna Sen to express well the degeneration of the colonial India and the emergence of the gentry in independent India. The language of the film in more than one sense is English. While emotional identification is to be with the Anglo-Indian lady, the social point of view of narration matches the (more or less) equally English gentry of Calcutta. The perspective alternates between a British one and an Indian English one, as if to replicate the handing down of English to Indians by the British.

In R. K. Narayan's story "A Horse and Two Goats", an American sojourner in an Indian village is shown as having a conversation with an illiterate villager Muni. Some messages getting through to the mutually unintelligible interlocutors, by fluke and by unintended means, forms the central thread of the story. Narayan avoids translating Muni's Tamil into English. Muni speaks only through gestures and *yes*es and *no*s. As the story is *in English*, the words the American speaks during the conversation are perfectly clear to the reader, but Muni must remain incommunicado because he has no English. Narayan exploits this unenviable linguistic situation in order to align his readers effortlessly with the American *and* his point of view, an alignment English makes possible. At the same time, however, it is not true that the reader always identifies with the American. The readers' sympathies are allowed to oscillate between the know-nothing American and his Indian counterpart, while they themselves can rest content with their "know-all" English.

Through the Anglo-Indian fiction of Ruskin Bond and Allan Sealy, "original" English characters have migrated into the present-day English writing too. A story by Manjula

Padmanabhan "The Copper-Tailed Skink" is a random example for a more recent use of an outsider as a character in Indian English fiction for the sake of a more "English" perspective. This is the story of the Indian experience of a European biologist Madeleine, who discovers a new species in the village of Devanahalli. Although this character is not the narrator, the narrator closely simulates her thought process to describe India. From this story one gets the impression that a story in English must have an "English" point of view. One may also begin to doubt if it is not the duty of an Indian writer in English to delude himself into imaginining that he *is* "English" before sitting down to write. India, it may seem, cannot be described in English without this purely imagined "English" perspective. In Padmanabhan's story the two Indian characters are Madeleine's colleague Mr Rao and his wife. The picture of Mr Rao is drawn in the usual stereotypical colours, making him too inquisitive and nosey.

> In five minutes Rao will be here, she thought. Eight hundred and fifty million Indians in India, and I have to be working with only one who is *always* on time. Like a precision chronometer, she thought, as if he doesn't exercise any choice in his punctuality, as if it is hard-wired into his system. [. . .] After all, the point of having a quality is when you can choose not to have it. She smiled to herself, faintly. Such a European idea, that! Not Indian at all.
>
> In India – or so it seemed, given her three month acquaintance – the aim appeared to be to make automata of everyone, eradicate the whole tiresome issue of choice altogether. (195–6)

The tone is one of generalised condemnation of Indians as unselfed and unmodern in their failure to exercise free choice. The culture shock of the European is expressed thus:

> The subcontinent seemed to tick away according to a schedule set by a handful of naked sages in some bygone era. And whenever you asked any questions about why something was done in a particular way or

why it couldn't be done in some other way, the answer, through howsoever roundabout a route, always came back to: "But . . . it is our *tradition*! Our *custom*. Our *habit*." Or whatever else. No effort at thought or change. (196)

Invectives tumble forth from Padmanabhan's pen: India is "the reproductory behemoth" and the people have a restrictive and repressive morality. At the mention of Madeleine's friend Jeremy's arrival, Mr Rao refers to him as "she", since an Indian does not expect a man to come and stay with a woman he is not married to. "Despite his Ph. D. his [Mr Rao's] English was atrocious" (198). In India, all places are unhygienic: "It seemed that he [Jeremy] had acquired the infection from the sandwiches he had eaten at the airport while waiting with all the other stranded passengers for the situations to normalise in the city" (206).

The history of India is just an incidental backdrop to the protagonists' lives – the assassination of Indira Gandhi affects them because of the inconvenience caused to them by its tumultuous aftermath. Finally the same character, who holds all these views about India, rises to be the epitome of kindness and humaneness by releasing the animal she had caught for study. In this story, it is worth wondering whose narrative voice the readers are invited to identify and sympathise themselves with. The answer is, obviously, the European's. At the moment of this story being read there comes into being the understanding and agreement between the two poles of Indian English literary communication – the English writer and the reader. All that the writer does here is to succumb to the temptation of adopting a readily available template-like point of view while writing the story in English. This stands in sharp contrast with R. K. Narayan's "A Horse and Two Goats" where the outsider's perspective is well balanced with a dialogic distribution of sympathies. The attention is drawn to the hard

Indian realities in a neutral non-pejorative manner, which Manjula Padmanabhan fails to do.

THE EXTERNAL POINT OF VIEW

We can see that English endows its Indian speaker with a sense of superiority over the speakers of other languages. Also, the less locally-bound and international quality of English enables its speakers to speak with a detachment towards the subject of their speech. That is, compared to the use of an Indian language, English will have a less culturally-specific range of reference. For example, if someone speaks about religion in an Indian language, he is most likely to be taken for an ignorant premodern believer or a fundamentalist, or one with a similar "agenda". But if he uses English to utter the same content, he is more likely to be exempted. This is hardly just an unimportant and natural feature of the Indian multilingual situations. Any difference that the use of English makes should be carefully noted, in order to see in perspective the depth and width and impact of its social penetration in India. For English in India today is a large enough language to have spawned a distinct culture in its wake. One can study the worldview characterising the Indian English culture by taking its fiction, films, journalistic writings, cartoons and television programmes as indices of a greater common mindset.

Stereotypes about India circulate within the country no less than they are popular abroad, and the culture of English here abounds in them. Hence, in Indian English literature and films we can frequently come across the repetition of one or the other preconceived idea or image about the non-English-speaking Indian. These stereotypes often come handy for writers and directors to compose jokes. A film like *Bollywood Calling* relies entirely on the "ridiculous" aspects of Indian popular culture. One common butt of ridicule, as seen earlier, is the poor speaker of English. The manners (lack of manners) associated with him/her are a lasting source of fun for the highly literate. The case of director Subrahmanyam in *Bollywood Calling* once again serves as the best example. He explains the storyline of his film to the American actor in the following English:

> Indians love all emotions in a single film. This story . . . about two brothers. When father mother take train journey, dacoits attack train. Dacoits – robbers, thieves. Killed mother, take son. Son becomes dacoit. Father sad. He goes to ashram, marries foreigner, comes to America. Second son born. He becomes computer engineer, mentally joined with the Indian dacoit brother. When Indian dacoit brother in trouble, he send signal to foreign brother. Both brothers join. With lot of romance, emotions songs, fights. . . . Not liking it . . . eh? (Quoted from the film)

It is important to observe the kind of mind that will derive laughter from this speech. There are two Americans in the scene besides Subrahmanyam – Pat Stormare the actor and his agent. Subrahmanyam's ways seem as outlandish to them as his story. The audience's point of view during this scene will match that of the Americans, and they will find the ungrammatical and mispronounced English of Subrahmanyam laughable. What shows through the making of this episode of innocent fun is proof of the self-congratulating confidence of the Indian English community that they are "Englished" enough and equal to the "real English" Americans in finding the "typical Indian" manners ridiculous. It also reveals the social chemistry of humour in Indian English films. People like Subrahmanyam give the Indian English-speakers a chance to once again denounce the "low taste" associated with formulaic Hindi films that they are too advanced and refined to like.

More examples are easy to find in various media where the complacency of the English-operated Indian psyche is evident. The well-known Indian English poet Nissim Ezekiel wrote "Goodbye Party to Miss Pushpa T. S." making an appeal to the same sensibility. This poem invites its readers to laugh at the unidiomatic and un-English English of an Indian.

Friends,
our dear sister
is departing for foreign
in two three days,
and
we are meeting today
to wish her bon voyage.

You are all knowing, friends,
what sweetness is there in Miss Pushpa.
I don't mean only external sweetness
but internal sweetness.
Miss Pushpa is smiling and smiling
even for no reason
but simply because she is feeling.

Miss Pushpa is coming
from very high family
Her father was renowned advocate
in Bulsar or Surat
I am not remembering now which place

Surat? Ah, yes,
Once only I stayed in Surat
with family members
of my uncle's very old friend
his wife was cooking nicely . . .
that was long time ago.

Coming back to Miss Pushpa
She is most popular lady
with men also and ladies also
whenever I asked her to do anything,
She was saying, "Just now only
I will do it." That is showing
good spirit. I am always
appreciating the good spirit
Pushpa Miss is never saying no.
Whatever I or anybody is asking
She is always saying yes,
and today she is going
to improve her prospect
and we are wishing her bon voyage.

Now I ask other speakers to speak,
and afterwards, Miss Pushpa
will do summing up. (190–191)

Although neither Ezekiel nor his many commentators pose this crucial question, we must. Is the voice speaking English, or is it speaking *in* English? Of course Ezekiel and his privileged readers would claim that they "speak English" (presumably like any white man or woman of the Anglo-American world), but the lesser beneficiaries of colonialism only, or try to, speak *in* English. Ezekiel's "very Indian poem" perhaps has no other message to deliver. The frequent use of progressive tenses is common in Indian languages unlike in English. This highly exaggerated example of what is known as "interference" in linguistics once again illustrates the humorous and self-critical approach with which English interprets Indian reality.

To cite another example, in *Mumbai Matinee*, we have the "baba" and his secretary, who lure people with advertisements of magical solutions to their problems in life. The formula of comedy is nothing new. It works through a displacement of things from their traditionally appointed contexts to new ones in order to produce incongruity. The fortune telling, black magic, hypnotism and supernatural abilities once associated with babas are displaced to a modern context where the sorcery will be exposed as trickery by virtue of its very modern context. Here, the baba is shown to be using a cell phone, promoting himself with printed advertisements, camping at a hotel called "Piccadilly", charging his customers through credit card and speaking English – practices that are unbecoming of a conventional baba. The viewer of *Mumbai Matinee* is of course a modern Indian who readily recognises the baba to be an impostor, again assuming incorrectly that the "modern" necessarily contradicts religion and superstition.

This standing apart, or taking an external point of view, is more widespread than this. A popular programme in MTV India, *Fully Faltoo*, draws upon similarly exaggerated traits of public personalities and celebrities. It features look-alikes of politicians, cine actors and cricketers in comic situations that are usually parodies of well-known scenes from Hindi films. The MTV mandarins are the urban Indians and the allegiance of their sensibility to "English" is evident and expected, given that it is the channel that pioneers the promotion of "Hinglish" in India.

In newspaper cartoons one frequently comes across the depiction of nativist types and rural Indian politicos as clowns: Laloo Prasad Yadav, for example. Perceived to be a man from the village, he is often shown in the vicinity of animals and speaking a "non-standard" dialect of Hindi. For the English language publications and their middle-class urban readers, Laloo Yadav typifies the primitive unmodern India. There is all the more reason for caricaturing Laloo in this fashion, given the fact that he is, with the other Yadav from U. P., a vocal leader of the "banish English" movement in Indian politics.

The satire, parody, ridicule and jokes, all arising from a perceived sense of superiority, in different forms of Indian English expression, have, towards the more contemporary period, come to be concentrated in the visual media. Films, cartoons and advertisements are the commonest vehicles of parody today. Even in fiction, when this kind of parody appears, it is the films that are parodied. Shashi Tharoor's novel *Show Business* is very close to the film *Bollywood Calling* when it makes fun of the formulaic Hindi film. Written as a film is seen on

the screen, the novel adopts a mock-serious voice to satirise the Bollywood films. It gives English translations for the usual songs, rendering them extremely ridiculous.[4] The implication is that the readers of Tharoor's novel will not enjoy the simplistic, sentimental and clichéd Hindi film, but identify with the author's point of view to dismiss them as silly.

The complete isolation or segregation of the lower/upper middle class of India based on their English language proficiency may be convenient, but hardly tenable. From our experience it should be evident that the "regular" audience for Bollywood and regional film includes moderate to very highly educated Indians, among them members of the civil services, school/college/University teachers, corporate officials of various ranks, and above all the educated college-going and unemployed youth of India. This, in turn, as I have argued elsewhere in the book, accounts for the very frequent use of words, concepts and ideology we generally ascribe to the English-educated urban elite: words like "mafia" and "black money"; concepts like "hero" and "villain"; "tragedy" and "comedy"; ideological constructs like "militancy", "police encounter", "dowry-death", "joint-family", "patriarchal order", etc. Thus *Show Business* succeeds, as does *Bollywood Calling*, in highlighting and privileging the Indian English sensibility over that of the common Hindi film spectator. Similarly, in *Midnight's Children*, Rushdie parodies the films Dev Anand used to make in the 1960s and 70s calling them "eastern-western" since these films showed Anand in the dress of a cowboy ("Gai-Wallah") and had stories equally divided into parts that happen in India and parts situated in America or Britain (49).

THE TOURIST APPROACH AND THE "DISCOVERY" OF INDIA

How India is represented in English changes with the genre of the description. That is, the form of representation changes the manner of presentation. In some genres, it constitutes one type of external point of view, namely, the tourist approach. In this common tone of Indian English, the neutrality to the content so exceeds the normal level that it becomes easily identifiable as a piece of Indian English writing/speech/language. Most Indian writing in English is vulnerable to this hyper-neutrality syndrome. The writers usually exaggerate to themselves the untranslatability of their own culture when they are using English and add unnecessary explanation and copious translation. The writers' relation to the reader, even when both are Indians, would resemble, from the tone of the writing, that between a guide and a tourist. This overly self-conscious manner of speaking, therefore, may be called another form of the external point of view.

On the Discovery Channel, one finds the programme *Discover India*, a weekly documentary series in English about the cultural diversity of the subcontinent. Every episode takes up a new place, a new ritual or a new community in India, and offers a comprehensive description of it. Intended for the English-knowing Indian, the narrative voice speaks as if to an outsider who is eponymously "discovering" India for the first time. The ultra-objectivity of this programme, or any other of the many modelled after it (*ndyah!* on the National Geographic Channel), leaves undisturbed the religious, communal, political, cultural and secular sentiments of the viewers that the use of an Indian language would ordinarily have hurt. Before dismissing this way of seeing India as a mere borrowed eye, one should remember that in Indian English, the borrowed eye virtually becomes the natural eye, and is functional in the sense that its range is pan-Indian and it can cater to the whole of India simultaneously as the Discovery Channel does.

The Sunday magazines of English newspapers extend into print the "Discovery" kind of tourist gaze. They cover themes like expatriate writers, vintage Hollywood, Indian classical music and dance, cuisine from different states, satellite television programmes, and include a regular column on travel. Even when an Indian destination is described, the details are presented as if addressed to an outsider, in an open invitation to "discover" India. The broad tendency is to familiarise and approximate things with the help of foreign and more "English" categories (by actually defamiliarising them). In a typical piece of Indian English film-journalistic writing Dev Anand often becomes "the Gregory Peck of India", Mani Ratnam and Mohan Lal, respectively, the "Spielberg" and "Robert de Nero" of India. One cannot recognise even Kalidasa except as the "Shakespeare of India". This is a particularly subtle and interesting phenomenon when we consider the "complex fate" of English in

India. Of the many roles English plays in India is the special role of a mediator (with the double senses of metamedia, and of a village explainer and "connector" among the half-educated clientele of Indian cities). How else would the young Indian know, unless explained by a reporter in a knowing parenthesis that Kapila Vatsyayan is no relative of the Vatsyayana of *Kamasutra*? The same principle is at work in honorific metaphors (the bubbly girl of the Hindi movies as "our Julia Roberts"!) that explain to and relate our less-knowing audience to our own cultural icons. A description is added wherever unintelligibility is vaguely suspected – if Ganapati is mentioned, "the elephant-god" will not be far behind in the text. While Tyagaraja invariably requires the phrase "the saint composer of Karnatic music" by way of introduction, Beethoven, Bach and Mozart, or even Janacek or Vivaldi can pass off without any such qualification – wrongly ascribing to the reader a supposed familiarity with the European composer and assuming him/her to be totally ignorant of Tyagaraja's music. Ironically, the explanation in fact requires more explanation than what it explains.

While examining the social life of English in creating a virtual India, one cannot ignore the language called "Hinglish", as it is an important channel for the spread of the tourist approach. Images of India available through "Hinglish" (most of the Indian English films are in this hybrid language) also have a deficiency of detail and are simplified for easy consumption. Therefore we find a host of essentialised stereotypes in visual and verbal media of contemporary India. Pictures that can be easily associated with India recur ad infinitum. In one of the early "indipop" songs, the singer heroine of the video is shown to choose an Indian hero for herself, rejecting many international suitors. In the background, and throughout the sequence, one sees a parade of yoga practitioners, kathakali performers, snakes, tigers, magic caskets and sorcerers – a random selection from the commonest "riches" of India. Remarkably, the refrain of the song is in English: "Made in India . . . made in India . . .". This album had a major role in founding and popularising the "Hinglish" culture in the metros. Interestingly, many Hindi film songs that are patriotic and enumerate the virtues of the country have English refrains like "I love my India" (*Pardes*) and "East or West, India is the best" (*Judwa*).

There is a more intellectual form of the external perspective as seen in a section of the Indian English fiction. The protagonist of this type of fiction will begin to have a reappraisal of India either after a travel abroad or through association with a foreigner. One example would be Pankaj Mishra's *The Romantics*, which belongs to the "East-West" sub-genre. In *Midnight's Children*, Rushdie speaks in this adopted tone about an India that he thinks is imaginary:

> A nation which had never previously existed was about to win its freedom, catapulting us into a world, which, although it had five thousand years of history, although it had invented the game of chess and traded with Middle Kingdom Egypt, was nevertheless quite imaginary: into a mythical land, a country which would never exist except by the efforts of a phenomenal collective will – except in a dream we all agreed to dream: it was a mass fantasy shared in various degrees by Bengali and Punjabi, Madrasi and Jat [. . .]. India, a new myth – a collective fiction in which anything was possible, a fable rivalled only by the two mighty fantasies: money and God. (111)

The speaker of these lines is an insider as well as an outsider. He is describing the intimate history of India from inside while fully utilising the advantage of distance inbuilt in the *language* he adopts.

NOTES

1. For a discussion of the typical ambience of the Indian English world see Chapter 4.

2. It should be noted that this comic character's name is Subrahmanyam, suggesting a south Indian cultural background, which a hero or a serious character in usual Indian English films will never have. Refer to the section on the typical names among the Indian English community (Chapter 5).
3. The aged Muslim couple in *Mr and Mrs Iyer* is an example of a non-English-influenced India that is still respectable. The couple's reaction to the exhibitive dress of a young college girl is one more instance of the tradition versus modernity theme.
4. This is another example for the comic formula of contextual displacement.

CHAPTER 4

From Word to Image, and Back

We already saw that there is a clear *point of view* in Indian English fiction and films, and in urban Indian life in general, for which English is responsible. The phrase *point of view* is very relevant while we discuss the social life of English in India. So far I have discussed the ways of understanding and describing India *through* the medium of English: that is, how the medium modifies the message. I now propose to take up some new dimensions of the act of *visualising* India through English. It will help us understand a significant *correspondence* between Indian English fiction and film, and the society. By this we also hope to better know the English Indian.

The "picture" of India we get from Indian English writing differs significantly from that in literatures in Indian languages. Likewise, films in Indian English create an impression about India which does not match what Hindi, Marathi or Tamil films make one think of India. At the same time, both fiction and film *in English* are highly similar. Apart from the similarities of stories and themes, the "pictures" found in Indian English fiction and films correspond closely to each other in a most literal sense also. This means that the verbal pictures of fiction are similar to, and tend to be, the visible pictures of films. The fiction of recent times has become more and more cinematic. The locales of these fictions – the home, office, parties, restaurants, interiors of cars, etc. – all part of city life on the move, are the likeliest locales of most of contemporary cinema too. The abundance of objects, sounds and colour, we can say, is common to fiction, film and city life today. Day-to-day life has begun to share with cinema the frequent change of background and a general avoidance of stillness. This is to deny that cinema merely "represents", "imitates" or "reflects" society. Instead, cinema and society are mutual and influences.

The speed and variety, the ephemeral public and private events, and the increasing virtuality of metropolitan life have rendered our lives, ifsoever metaphorically, cinematic. Many other associate devices of cinema that equally carry the cinema effect – like television, sensational newspapers, tabloids, cartoons, advertisements, and film and lifestyle magazines, whose chief matter is the visual – are immeasurably formative to the public imagination today. Borrowing from cinema its three defining features (without acknowledgement in many cases), visual, fictional and narrative, all these media have collectively set a broader stage for cinema by making it overflow into lifestyles in general. The aim of this essay is to analyse the operation of English as the facilitating metamedium of all the above media. More importantly, the purpose is to present more evidence for this from the analysis of the correspondence between Indian English films and Indian English fiction.

The vocabulary of our description here abounds in words related to vision, sight and perception. Critical imagery of this kind not only becomes unavoidable, but is the very purpose of the discussion because the subject is "visual culture" in India and its maintenance in the country through the English language. The blurring of the boundaries between fiction and film, journalism and film, and urban life and film is neither very new nor to be studied as something newly introduced to our culture. This phenomenon has irrevocably merged into private and public lives the world over. All major English newspapers of India have daily pullouts featuring mainly photos related to films, fashion and the culture industry, feeding to the voyeuristic appetite of the masses. News, snippets and gossip from

Hollywood and Bollywood find a common venue on the sheets of these papers. The treatment of Hollywood is as though it were a natural part of Indians' idea about films, while most Indians do not watch Hollywood films. The ones who do are unmistakeably the urban Indians who have the cultural competence (procured through English) to appreciate these films. They also form a part of the audience for Indian cinema. Interestingly, the most popular film magazine on Hindi cinema, *Filmfare*, is an English publication, and so is *Stardust*.[1] English therefore proves itself to be the language of information and literature on cinema in general for the urban masses. Many an Indian glossy magazine is proof enough for the fact that English has emerged as the medium for disseminating "lifestyle". It is possible to relate Indian English films and Indian English fiction in this cultural context as commonly sourced by the prospering social life of English. The most recent reason for including fiction here as a component of visual culture is a graphic novel named *Corridor* by Sarnath Banerjee published in 2004. It offers a firm proof for the amalgamation of the visual and the word, fiction and film, inside the Indian English culture.

A VISUAL NOVEL

The famous American critic of the novel Leslie A. Fiedler once remarked that the "art novel", or the avant-garde Modernist novel, signalled the death of the novel. He meant that the novel was no longer a literary form for the masses, which it originally was. Its rebirth, according to him, consists in the more recent spurt of popular novels that restore to the genre its initial purpose of entertaining the common people. Along with these remarks, he makes the following interesting and valid observation on the visual character of recent fiction:

> It is a characteristic of new-Pop, or Popular fiction in a post-cinematic age that at its most authentic it constitutes, as it were, the embryonic form of a film – words on the page being [. . .] often just a transitional stage on the way toward the even more broadly available narrative form of images on screen. (200)

In our day, Fiedler would have only more reasons to say what he said about the abundant visuality that has invaded fiction in print. The cognitive habits of the people have changed vastly because of the vast changes in the media of communication and expression. As if to demonstrate this in black and white, Sarnath Banerjee published a piece of experimental visual fiction, called *Corridor* in 2004.

Described by a commentator as India's first graphic novel (*The Hindu*, May 30, 2004), *Corridor* is a multi-plot novel that tells the story of a young man Brighu, bred on Phantom comics, and western literature and music, who seeks a love life in Delhi and Kolkata. The other plots include the lives of Shintu, a newly-married man in search of an aphrodisiac that will liven up his sex life, Dr D. V. D. Murthy, an English literature enthusiast, and Digital Dutta, a computer professional. In the words of another reviewer, *Corridor* "is a book that is created like a comic strip, the text and images woven to create a single piece of work. It has the depth of a novel and the visual characteristics of a film, 'a medium through which several complex layers of story telling can be achieved'" (Tanya Abraham, *The Week*, May 30, 2004, 64). The narration of each story is at some stage interrupted to include another story introducing a new set of characters. This intercutting of the sequence is immediately reminiscent of a cinematic narrative which is characterised by immediate change of scene, setting and mood. The novel-film starts with Brighu's search for a book in the bookshops of Connaught Place in Delhi. As soon as the scene is unfolded, the narrative lapses into a five-page flashback during which

Brighu is introduced as a collector of obsolescent things like a Rotring pen, old LP records, Phantom comics, etc. From the slideshow of Delhi life that follows, we learn the life of Jehangir Rangoonwalla the bookseller, whose past is also presented in flashback. In the three pages that contain the reminiscences of Rangoonwalla, the pictures have a deep shade simulating black and white (see picture on the right). Unmistakeably, it is the cinematic way of thought that pictures the past in black and white as though the world itself lacked colour at the historical time when there were no means to represent it in colour. Films themselves often adopt this technique of referring to the past by means of a black-and-white flashback. Who could conceive of Mahatma Gandhi in colour, or imagine the Indian struggle for Independence in technicolour? When Gandhiji was assassinated in January 1948, Nehru famously announced this national misfortune to a crowd of black apparitions gathered at

Nehru announcing Gandhi's death (*The Hindu*, 6 Aug 2004)

From *Corridor*, 38

the Birla House in New Delhi on a surreal black-and-white night through the camera of Henri Cartier-Bresson (see picture on page 78). A few months before that, when the Indian tricolour replaced the Union Jack on the mast, it was no more than a bicolour. Black and white thus became a metaphoric marker for the past whereby the vehicle was the history of cinema and the tenor, history itself. It is certainly a phase in the moulding of actuality in the image of virtuality as suggested by the late Jacques Derrida (in *Echographies of Television*) resulting in "artifactualiy" and "activirtuality" (3). From this simple choice of black and white to represent the past, one discovers that the contemporary man's psychic activities have the semblance of cinema. One asks whether today's mind, after decades of unconscious familiarisation, is not patterned after the grammar and inflectional modes of the institutions of the visual such as television, photography, cinema, paintings, etc. Is not cinema ingrained in the modern mind as the unconscious organiser of mind's images? This should be the case of nature (mind) getting shaped in the image of culture (visual) – one can only modestly theorise.

There is little wonder that our novels resemble films. Digital Dutta of *Corridor* is a software professional torn between his Marxist intellectual upbringing and a desire for a visa to America. Dutta's story is followed by that of Shintu, the newly-married, who suspects that he has erectile dysfunction. Dr D. V. D. Murthy is unable to get rid of from around himself the smell of corpses he operates on every day. The interspersing of many narratives and scenes in this manner, however, may not be "new" in fiction at all. At the level of form, the contemporary novel is always already cinematic, as Fiedler noted. But cinema and the visual in general – images that have fictional or historical content, or both – have another function at the level of content or "meaning" in a novel like *Corridor*. The image inventory of our culture is full of ideas and images from films. They come very handy to Indian English writers and filmmakers who fit them into different social contexts in their works. A study of this process of image adaptation will give us a clear understanding of some of the basic formulas of these genres. We can also see how English as their medium matters in the whole process.

PHOTOGRAPHIC CONTENT

The American election process that was to culminate in Kennedy becoming president in 1961 was notable for the role the circulating images played in the President's success. The mandate proved in a definitive way the power of the photographic image to transmit a lot of messages with minimum help from explicit language. A widely publicised photograph at that time was a half-length profile shot of Kennedy, his eyes looking upward and hands joined together. Roland Barthes discusses this photograph in his essay "The Photographic Message". He explains how this Kennedy photograph meant in the context of the election.

> Here it is the very pose of the subject [Kennedy] which prepares the reading of the signifieds of connotation, youthfulness, spirituality, purity. The photograph clearly only signifies only because of *the existence of a store of stereotyped attitudes which form readymade elements of signification* (eyes raised heavenward, hands clasped). A historical grammar of iconographic connotation ought to thus look for its material in painting, theater, association of ideas, stock metaphors, etc., that is to say, precisely in "culture". (201) (Italics are mine.)

(As irony would have it, Kennedy was the first head of a modern state who was literally "shot into fame" by his assassin Oswald. The widely circulated photograph of the murder did this too.)

"The existence of a store of stereotyped attitudes which form readymade elements of signification" is what helps Sarnath Banerjee's *Corridor* make sense to its reader. The early reviews have held the novel to be a portrait of various aspects of modern life from sexuality and morality to urban angst. One only needs to add that this *angst* is not pan-Indian but that of the English-educated Indian. Advertising effects apart, the early criticism does make, probably unintentionally, a point that can only be more subtly arrived at. Irrespective of what it is for the author, and his reviewers, for a percipient analyst of Indian English fiction, *Corridor* presents a view of the urban English-speaking India and its mindsets. Consider the following: along with his cartoons, Banerjee uses numerous photographs that relay voluminous cultural and historical meanings. To describe Digital Dutta's personality, Banerjee sets photos of Hitchcock, Pele, Nusrat Fateh Ali Khan, Harry Houdini, Einstein, Nehru, Groucho Marx, Bruce Lee, etc. around the head of Dutta (see picture). In another part of the novel, Digital Dutta is shown to be a communist by placing around his head photos of Stalin, Jyoti Basu, Mao, Lenin, Subhash Chandra Bose and Ernesto Che Guevara. D.V. D. Murthy, on the other hand, recites lines from John Keats's "Ode to a Nightingale". These images begin to mean in the way Barthes suggested, drawing on the "culture" of metropolitan "English" Indians, as soon as they come into contact with the cognitive instruments of the readers from this community. In the process of making sense, the images start to *correspond* to "the readymade elements of signification" present in that culture, which is also their destination. For confirmation, it will be useful to remember here what we saw in the first chapter as the sources of the cultural mindset of metropolitan India.

CINEMA AS CONTENT

The tradition of cinema establishes certain easily identifiable stereotypes whose invocation will readily introduce the

From *Corridor*, 41

connotations clichéd in them. The Barthesian paradigm of cultural signification finds numerous examples in *Corridor*. One among them: The face of actor Lalita Pawar has come to stand for the cruel stepmother or mother-in-law, the conspiring servant, and the evil, domineering woman in general. This novel uses the face of Lalita Pawar to refer comically to the sexually unfulfilled woman who turns to henpecking (see picture). Banerjee amusedly provides the reader with subject for readymade laughter, little realising the potentially offensive sexist messages.

In "The Degree of Anglicisation and the External Point of View" (Chapter 3) I have described how the Indian English mind laughs at the very stereotypes of Hindi cinema it also enjoys with a willing suspension of rationality. We have seen films like *Bollywood Calling* and novels like *Show Business* do

From *Corridor*, 63

this. The use of images from films in *Corridor* is also an instance of this: deriving fun from the folly of those (the masses) who continue to relish the clichés. The English-knowing and culturally competent urban Indian is indescribably delighted that he has such a big horde of unrefined inferiors. In short, we have a whole range of ideas that have become laughable in the light of modern rational thought. Another film of this fiction/ film-on-film type is *The King of Bollywood* (2004), an Indian English movie starring Om Puri in the role of an exaggerated film hero. Today the occurrence of these stock ideas and types in Indian English fiction and film makes for a double stereotype. The mockery of clichés in Hindi films has become another clichéd act within the specific circles (of English) where they evoked fun, but no longer do. This has merely turned into an all-too-familiar formula in Indian English films and fiction. The image from films commonly deployed in the writing and films in English in India hence have the nature of a double stereotype – a stereotype stereotyped as a stereotype. We wonder whether two negatives add up to a positive and reinforce the stereotype that can no longer be laughed at.

In the sub-section "The External Point of View" I have illustrated the patterned way of understanding Indian society in fiction, film and writing in general. But it does seem pertinent to reinvoke this stereotyping because it relativises the culture of English and that of other Indian languages, and makes the distinction in social attitudes more visible. Although no longer interesting as a source of entertainment, the comic types of Indian English fiction and films are sample enough to deduce the perceived or actual "superiority" of English in the pecking order of languages in India. Rural India is ridiculed in many ways; one example is a song "Welcome to India" composed by two Indian students of an American university.

WELCOME TO INDIA

Yaa, MC Vikram and Luda Krishna representing y'all,
That's right . . . increase the volume please . . . thank you.
Welcome to India, mango juices and *lassis*, *samosa* crazy *desis*
and little kids that are milking the *bhainses*.
Yaa, MC Vikram and Luda Krishna representing y'all,
That's right . . . increase the volume please . . . thank you.
Toothbrush in my pocket, what is that?
We use our fingers here to keep our teeth so clear, who said that?
Luda Krishna here, Vikram pulling the *Tata* gears,
and I am sitting in the *Maruti Supreme*
with the cooling glass on no one bothers me,
biggest stars since the ever famous *Mamooty*.
Come with me to a place where we sip *Frooties*,
and we eat the sweets while monkeys roam the streets.
Old uncle sits – big bellies and burps smelly (burp!)
Thank you Vikram, would you please pass the jelly,
I mean the pickle, hand it down this way . . . *Namaste*
we greet the people as they enter the train!
Sixty-five people hanging out, the doors start coming out.
Therefore, please don't raise your hand, you are not sure.
I walked into the local corner-store,
bought myself a very nice looking carroms board.
My fingers get sore when I shoot and I score,
and the *ladkis* all scream coz they all want some more,
of the Luda Krishna and the Vikram MC,
Sweetest thing to hit the States since mango *chutney*.
We keep the *kundis* shaking, you better trust me.
The name is Luda Krishna, but my friends call me Thambi, watch!! (burp!)
Ohhh, Vikram, is that you my friend?!
That is me my friend!
Oh, please enter this rap game!
Ok man! C'mon . . . tell me where you're going my friend.

Welcome to India where the cows eat hay,
and we drive auto-rickshaws everyday,
Goat meats, yummy sweets, wild monkeys roaming,
The roosters don't crow till five in the morning! (2x)
Now the *kundis* don't jiggle till I'm rapping,
So please don't pass the gas when you're laughing.
Up the music charts like mango trees I climb,
With a smooth voice like mine, is it a crime?
Representing FOB-iness since ninety-seven
Rap *maharaja*, I don't work at 7-Eleven.
Throw your hands in the air if you've got facial hair,
Not just for the guys, c'mon ladies be fair!
I'm the MFP – Most FOB-ious Player,
Wearing hot *lungis*, do you think I really care?
Monday night – computer club
Tuesday night – at Akbaar grocery saying "Sweet thang, what is up?"
Wednesday – I'm out making rupees
Thurday – On lookout for Bharatnatyam queen
Friday – Everybody must know where I'm at, coz I'm chilling on the field with my big cricket bat.
Saturday – my farts are breezy . . . believe me, so strong they will get you mad dizzy,
Sunday – Yaar, I cannot start weeping because on Monday I will start the
Creeping – Hallo!
Ohhhh . . . I love that my friend!
Yaa dawg, that was a funda-stic. Hey thank you, you're fabulous!
Oh, thank you my friend! Oh . . .
Welcome to India where the cows eat hay,
and we drive auto-rickshaws everyday,
Goat meats, yummy sweets, wild monkeys roaming,
The roosters don't crow till five in the morning! (2x)
Oh, oh, go Luda, go Luda.
Ah, it's my birthday!
That is your birthday, man!

Yaaaaah. You go boy!
Oh oh oh . . . it's great!
Ah, Indian honor my friend. Good night!
All right, goodbye . . . kiss my buttocks!!

(The song is reproduced from a web page *www.andrew.cmu.edu/user/gkumar/WelcomeToIndia.htm*)

This is our new-century version of Nissim Ezekiel's "Goodbye Party to Miss Pushpa T. S." and perhaps of the songs in the novel *Show Business* to be quoted presently.

A predecessor to *Corridor* in using cinema as form as well as content is Shashi Tharoor's *Show Business* (1991). The novel tells the story of a film hero Ashok Banjara along with the stories of many films he acted. The parts of the novel are named "Take One", "Take Two", etc., and many chapters have names of films as titles. The subject of *Show Business* is Indian cinema, its manner is satirical, and its formal organisation and narrative method make it a film shot in words and screened on the page. An excerpt can avoid a lengthy description of the novel: In what seems to be a parody of the traditional Indian ideas of familial bonding depicted in Hindi films, Tharoor writes for the novel a translation of a typical song which would have occurred in any Hindi film. In English translation, the meaning of the song is nothing less than ludicrous:

(*Refrain*)
We're one small happy family,
We live and love together.
We're one small happy family
In sunshine and bad weather.
The mother:
We're one small happy family,
Together we stand and fall.
We're one small happy family,

All for each and each for all.
(*Refrain*)
Ashok:
We're one small happy family,
United, good and strong.
We're one small happy family,
So nothing can go wrong.
(*Refrain*)
Maya:
We're one small happy family,
Looked after by our mother.
We're one small happy family,
Protected by brother.
(*Refrain*)
(25–26)

The convention of song and melodrama common in Hindi film looks absurd when it is recontextualised in English. The language one speaks determines the attitude one wears. The multilingual Indian relishes Bollywood flicks when he wears a Hindi identity, and laughs at the irrationality of it as soon as he dons a "neutral", "official", "modern", "sophisticated" English identity. It seems appropriate to attribute the successful coexistence of traditional culture and modernity in India to the diverse identities of Indians that can be switched into a pan-national identity of an English-knowing citizen, wherever a switching is needed. Such areas like higher education, politics, law and administration were already being driven by the modern part of the Indians' socio-psychic make. In culture this appears mixedly – in fiction, journalism, publications and films in English. The literary phenomenon of Indian English fiction and the recent visual media with English content, along with other areas of social life where English is the medium, prove an important thing about contemporary Indian society. When seen in perspective, all these phenomena prove the *autonomy* of

English language in India. In other words, English in India is increasingly on its own in such a manner as makes it eligible to be compared as an influential sub-culture to Spanish in Latin America.

VISUALISING LIFE AS FILM

Ready images, or stereotypes, from cinema are used in Indian English films simultaneously as they appear in fiction. In many films one can see a common and typical situation presented by reintroducing a famous previous instance of such a situation in films themselves. In Nagesh Kukunoor's *Rockford* (2000), the adolescent Rajesh Naidu, admitted to the Rockford school, develops a crush on his young school teacher played by Nandita Das. At the same time, the boy is worried that she is in love with his physical education teacher Johnny Mathew (Kukunoor). A daydream of Rajesh's goes like this: he and his teacher-girlfriend are singing the song *Shokhiyon mein khola jayein phoolon ka shabab* . . . and playfully chasing each other around a haystack as in the famous film *Prem Pujari*. Rajesh and the lady are dressed exactly like Dev Anand and Waheeda Rehman, and are at a place exactly like the village in *Prem Pujari*. All of a sudden, Rajesh disappears from the scene and is replaced by Johnny Mathew the fitness trainer, who resumes the song with the girlfriend.[2] The rude interruption of this sweet dream is avenged in another dream where Rajesh takes up a pistol and shoots his rival dead. The technique used here is the same as in *Corridor*, where stock idiomatic images serve the purpose of comic effect and cultural contextualisation. Also, in *Rockford*, the children are shown the *Dracula* film in their hostel, and Rajesh begins to have nightmares in which Dracula preys on him.

In *Bollywood/Hollywood* the comparison of life to films takes an explicit form, the title being suggestive of an equation that (from outside at least) life in India is what is seen in Bollywood films. Many references made by characters associating themselves with film characters, and their lives with situations in films are proof of this. In this film the hero Rahul's girlfriend dies in an accident, and he vows never to marry. The dramatic situation that follows involving Rahul, his mother, grandmother and brother resembles typical Hindi film drama. Rahul's young brother jokingly comments that his mother looks like Reema Lagoo and grandmother, like Zohra Sehgal – two actors identified as the typical mother and grandmother respectively of Hindi films. (Zohra Sehgal is an interesting and allusive case because Sehgal, almost alone in her histrionic talent and background, strides the two worlds of India and Britain, Hindi and English, theatre and film, "art" and "commerce".) The heroine's father, played by Kulbhushan Kharbanda, is a Punjabi patriot who sings the *Pardes* song "I love my India . . .". At this Sunita, his daughter, says, "Look at you fuming at the mouth like Amrish Puri from some Bombay film" (quoted from the film).

CINEMATIC METAFICTION

The erasure of genric boundaries between different forms of text is characteristic of postmodern culture. Never before have novels and films been so full of obsessive narcissism. Playful writers have taken liberties with the conventions of their genre, following the late twentieth-century theoretical opinion that meaning in a text is a matter of those very genric conventions. The meaning of a newspaper report, a television serial, a poem, a letter, a legal document, an obituary or a portrait wholly depends on the social institutions that provide them identity and public sustenance. As a consequence, the subject of art has become art itself, and its purpose, only to reveal the *artifice*.

Forms of art prefix *meta-* to their names as an attempt to stay contemporary and profess "knowing" themselves. The paradigm of self- and cross-reference and the uncertainty of genre can just as well be applied to the Indian fiction and films in English in order to demonstrate their definitive collaboration. Here we shall see how they have in common a way of referring to themselves and the conditions of their production. In other words, this will reveal how they are *correspondingly* metafictional.

In an earlier chapter we discussed the self-reflexivity of the English-sponsored culture in India with respect to novels and films in Indian English that are conscious of their medium. In them we saw that the medium of English mattered centrally in determining the ways of representing that culture as well as the content of representation. While discussing the film *Monsoon Wedding*, we concluded that a spontaneous reference in it to Arundhati Roy was an instance of the English-speaking Indians unconsciously recognising Indian English literature as *their* literature. In many novels and films, the range of historical and cultural references extended beyond Indian themes into an international repository of ideas: English literature, world affairs, Hollywood films, world literature, etc. To decode these messages one needs English, for their dissemination happens here chiefly through this medium. English delimits the boundaries of information. English as a handy tool growing into a pan-national intangible institution, and then into a distinct and prospering culture, is what this book seeks to illuminate. Instead of approaching a culture as a whole, I have examined its tangible embodiments in different forms of text: fiction, film, and writing in general. The interconnectedness and *correspondence* of these texts and their inevitable co-responses to the parent culture of Indian English are the subject of this book. To demonstrate this unambiguously, a little more evidence can be added by pointing out the metalepsis[3] of Indian English.

At one point the film *Monsoon Wedding* breaks the illusion of being fictional and proves itself to be closer to social reality than to mere fiction (in an overt acknowledgement of what one expects all fiction to actually do). At the marriage that is the climax of the film, the girl Ria (Shefali Shetty) lashes out at her uncle who had sexually abused her as a child. Peace and merriment are restored by turning this uncle out of the marriage party and from the house. Now, conventions of the story demand that Ria finds a "suitable" boyfriend, or better still, a husband. The film provides him to her in the form of Jas Aurora (actor), who arrives from abroad. As he appears on the screen, the audience hears in the background a very popular indipop song *Aaja nach ley . . . aaja nach ley*. In a music video with a similar Punjabi-pop song, *Ishq mita, hai, hai . . .*, the same Jas Aurora arrives from abroad to court Mallaika Arora (Khan). The Indian English film here blatantly alludes to its own associate phenomenon, the indipop music. By including what is actual, or by merging what are by public perception disparate fictional worlds, into one narrative, the film owns up the responsibility of having represented social truth on the fictional platform of film. This is just a more explicit instance of the widespread trans-textualisation of English-aided culture in India.

The next similar instance is the appearance of actor Akshay Khanna as himself at a marriage in the film *Bollywood/Hollywood*. This eponymous incident helps the film to show as actual a society and culture (the NRI community in Canada) in which film stars lead glorious off-screen lives. One way to read this is as an admission that the platform of film has been used to documentary effect, and the films themselves are the carriers of this confession.

On the other hand, the genres of writing and television that are believed to be the presenters of truth are full of apocryphal news described with utmost naturalism. The film-blitz journalism of the gossip media is produced to be consumed with one's eyes closed, with wishful imagination of actuality. Appropriating the fact-giving authority of print and the solemn podium of publication, fiction is freely imported with an uncanny attitude that has no respect for either truth or falsehood. Reproduced here is an article (see cutting) that appeared in the "Delhi Times" supplement of *The Times of India* on April 11, 2004 about "our Marilyn Monroe" Mallika Sherawat. The newspaper story (story!) corresponds to many a tale of an innocent girl's rise to stardom in an exploitative tinsel world. (It is a case of literal correspondence if we compare this article to the story of Karuna in Shobha De's *Socialite Evenings*, where a daughter of orthodox parents becomes a model). What is notable is that all these stories happen in and around films, and are told to us in English.

Besides all these, we may need further corroboration for Fiedler's hypothesis about novels and our own discovery of the cinematic in literature in Indian English before we can assert that this phenomenon is ubiquitous today. Rushdie's *The Satanic Verses* recurs here as an example. The expatriate author takes the help of popular films and blends it with his own *external* perspective to describe an Indian identity:

> "O my shoes are Japanese," Gibreel sang, translating the old song into English in semi-conscious deference to the uprushing host-nation, "These trousers are English, if you please. On my hand, red Russian hat; my heart is Indian for all that". (5)

More than *Midnight's Children*, *The Satanic Verses* is the book that adopts the camera to forge its own point of view. In the familiar metafictonal manner, the instrument of perception is included in the text under perception. As a tribute to the invading visual into fiction, a passage from the chapter "Mahound" reads:

> Gibreel: the dreamer, whose point of view is sometimes that of the camera and at other moments, spectator. When he's the camera, the pee

MANOJ KESHARWANI

Viagra & the Nun

A small town beginning and strict parents...Mallika Sherawat has left the restrictions behind to seduce the box-office, says Jyoti Sharma

Mom thrashed me when I first wore lipstick: My hometown? Rohtak, a small town in Haryana. A place where women and cattle are both kept in the backyard. My early days were a nightmare. I come from a traditional jat family. My father is a landlord and my mother still remains in *ghoonghat*. I tried to follow the standards set by my family, but my spirit always rebelled. I still remember the first time I applied lipstick. I was in Xth standard and was admiring myself in the mirror when my mother saw me. She was shocked and thrashed me badly.

Miranda College - my first pair of jeans! My family moved to Delhi after I completed my school. My first experience of a big city. I joined Miranda college as my father didn't want me to go to a co-educational institute. It was after moving to Delhi that I got my first pair of jeans. Despite my parents' opposition, I started modelling. But my real calling was always movies. My family was horrified at the suggestion. What followed was an ugly scene with my father where he broke all relations with me. My mother still loved me, but she was helpless. I decided to come to Mumbai.

Mumbai - I lived in a rat hole and cried myself to sleep: With that one train journey, I travelled over so many time zones. Suddenly I was in this strange city where I knew nobody. I was scared but everytime I thought about going back, I asked myself: Where will life be more difficult? For one-and-a-half years, I went around studios but all in vain. I was living in a rat hole apartment, away from my family. I also had to sell my most precious possession — a pair of earrings that my *nani* had given me. I cried that night and several other nights too...

AJIT NINAN

SUNDAY SPECIAL

insecure, terribly lonely.

Sex & Money drive the world: I soon realised this world is run by men, not God. The debate about women's emancipation is hogwash. While I went around looking for work, all I got were propositions. Living alone in Mumbai was not easy. I was asked to undress to survive in films. Today, the very people who made those rules accuse me of a skin show. I distrust people who badmouth sex and money. These are the two forces that drive our lives.

I wanna be a box office Viagra: My icon is Madonna and I refuse to conform to set standards. Today people are coming to watch *Murder* because of Mallika Sherawat. When I see my cutouts and hoardings, I feel a sense of triumph. I want to do even hotter movies, with more love scenes and more titillation. I want the audience to throw coins on the screen every time I appear. I want them to fall in front of my car, blow flying kisses and go berserk. I love it when they come to me and say, *Mallika murder kar diya* or *Mallika meri khwaish*. This is what I have always longed for. At the end of the day, I have worked like Viagra on a sluggish box office. My movies have killed the star system. People come to watch me and I have gatecrashed into this system.

In real life, I live like a nun: While my professional life is going great guns, I live like a nun personally. There is nobody in my life. I am on the lookout for a man who has more guts than I have.

From "Delhi Times" *The Times of India*, 11 April 2004

oh vee is always on the move, he hates static shots, so he's floating up on a high crane looking down at the foreshortened figures of the actors, or he's swooping down to stand invisibly between them, turning slowly on his heel to achieve a three-hundred-and-sixty degree pan, or maybe he'll try a dolly shot tracking along beside Baal and Abu Simbel as they walk, or handheld with the help of a steadycam, he'll probe the secrets of the Grandee's bedchamber. But mostly he sits up on Mount Cone like a paying customer in the dress circle, and Jahilia is his silver screen. He watches and weighs up the action like any movie fan, enjoys the fights infidelities moral crises, but there aren't enough girls for a real hit, man, where are the goddamn songs? They should have built up a fairground scene, maybe a cameo role for Pimple Billimoria in a show tent, wiggling her famous bazooms. (108)

* * *

In Indian English fiction and films, there is a particular way of *visualising* India that owes to the medium of English. As English selects and restricts the audience of these products, their life cycle, from production to consumption, and from further production to consumption in the manner of a tradition, takes place in the self-contained circle of English. This circle can be isolated and described in many more ways and with more detail than can be attempted here. The sociology, linguistics, history and economics of English language in India are all important in their own ways. The focus of this study has been the *culture* of English in India as it is *visible* in Indian English fiction and films. In the context of the two genres, the visualisation of India is also a *visual*-isation: a perceptible movement from the symbolic to the iconic. If all the rest of the correspondent phenomena whose medium is English are also taken into consideration, we can broadly see how they distribute the cinema effect to various walks of life.

NOTES

1. Many students of Indian English literature do not seem to know that Shobha De, an Indian English writer of "pop" fiction and weekly columns, once used to write for the *Stardust*. It was in these columns that she began her now-trademark style (code-mixed "Hinglish" whose special-effects include crosslingual puns, spelling-pronunciation and literal translation into English of Indian language expressions), which is now widely imitated by Indian English columnists and Indian English film script writers.
2. A scene reminiscent of *jaaneman, jaaneman* song sequence in *Chitchor*, where the film-watcher hero Amol Palekar substitutes Dharmendra (and Vidya Sinha, Hema Malini), etc.
3. Critic Gerard Genette in his *Narrative Discourse* (Ithaca: Cornell, 1980) introduces this term to mean the conscious violation of the limits of a narrative "level", as when the author himself appears in the novel in his own person.

CHAPTER 5

Correspondence and the New English India

I HAVE discussed the *correspondence* between Indian English fiction and Indian English film in three different senses. Corresponding as "communicating to each other", corresponding as "being analogous", and corresponding as "co-responding" or "answering together". In the first sense it is a dialogue between the two popular genres. Also, the shared themes, stories, character types, stock situations, comic formulae and a common point of view (the social ethos presented) make them kindred genres. This is the second form of correspondence I have addressed. A third and broader sense in which *correspondence* is used relates to the *social life of English in India.* Now the *correspondence* of Indian English fiction, Indian English film and English itself with one another should be put in perspective. What is the relevance of this correspondence? How does it matter to the general fate of our languages and culture? This concluding chapter is devoted to addressing these questions.

In the first chapter we saw that there was a considerably large urban audience for Hollywood films in the sixties and seventies. That generation took inspiration and models to emulate from English films from the West. The influence reflected visibly on their lifestyle and social behaviour. Indian films also imitated Hollywood in many ways – and films are a major influence on life in India. What many describe as "westernisation" has a subtle relationship to English-as-a-cultural-competence. There exists a direct proportion: the more English you have, the more "westernised" you are. The acquisition and command of English unites together a dominant class with its own distinct values, character, socio-political preferences and performance.

Indian English culture was gradually taking shape through the sixties and seventies. The circulation of English through various media from the nineteenth century onwards ensured its continuous expansion into newer arenas and uses. Indian English fiction defined itself as one of the world literatures in English. English matured into a suitable medium of self-expression for at least a class of Indians. Although there was much literature in English, there were few well-known Indian films in English apart from the Merchant–Ivory co-productions that had India-related themes. But they are hardly *Indian* English films.

As I have shown in detail in Chapter 1, English in independent India set apart a distinct class in society which seems to have developed its own lifestyles and ways of thinking. English itself, we can say, has made its speakers different from others, given the fact that the arrival of Enlightenment rationality to India was through English, and its spread was chiefly achieved through English. The architect of modern India, Jawaharlal Nehru, was a product of the Enlightenment spirit. The earliest works of modern Indian literature have amply documented the transformation of India through English and have even placed it as their central theme. O. Chandu Menon's *Indulekha* (1889), arguably the first Malayalam novel, assumes so important a position in literary history because it faithfully records the change in such enduring institutions as the family, marriage and the erstwhile matriarchy from a very "English" point of view. This was the first time the European literary form was being experimented in Malayalam, and Chandu Menon was a magistrate serving the British government.

In *Indulekha* we find a new English-educated generation rather impatient to replace the traditional clan system and embrace modernity. More than a century hence, the conflict of the new and old generations is still a theme in Indian English fiction and films. Now the source of rebellion of the young, English education itself, is not mentioned but taken for granted or accepted. And as we have seen in the section "The Generation Gap" in Chapter 2, the resistance of the contemporary conservatives is only feigned and is only another way of being supportive of the new.[1]

Today the change is taking place at a faster pace because of the spread of English-enabled teletechnologies. Morality has changed from the prescriptive to the accommodative. Of all times, today we have the maximum freedom of expression. And individualism, in the sense of choosing to live according to one's free will and rational action, is paramount. Today an increasing number of Indians choose to live in this way. I would argue that this emergent culture of English India is reflected in the *correspondent* genres of Indian English fiction and film. I have pointed out several instances of the difference of attitude between Indian language films and Indian English films, and exclusive speakers of Indian languages and English-speakers. On the one hand, we have a group of people subscribing to received ideas and prescriptive religions unquestioningly, and on the other, we have the English-speaking Indians who seem to have escaped the dogmas through reason, only to recite instead the chronic clichés of their own culture, which I have discussed in the section "The External Point of View". The excesses of the English-speakers seem to be pardonable – their hypocrisy, know-all attitude, etc. – because of a few welcome changes. The infirmities of English seem to be giving way to an *authentic* lifestyle and thinking with the many changes that are taking place worldwide. English has de-essentialised the Indian mind. The Indian I have consistently referred to in my writing as "the English-speaker" or the "English-conscious Indian" is largely free from the traditions of ancient religions and their values. Tradition and modernity are no longer binaries strictly enforced and argued for and against, but situationally adaptable collections of valuable human experience. If one is keen on describing causation, one can no doubt attribute it to postmodernity and the cultural revolution of "both . . . and" and "neither . . . nor" that supplanted the instrumental reason holding out through the language and logic of "either . . . or".

In an essay "Is There an Indian Way of Thinking", A. K. Ramanujan describes his father. His father was a mathematician and astronomer. He was a "south Indian Brahman gentleman". In his dress he combined the dhothi and turban with English serge jacket. His visitors and friends included both European mathematicians and local astrologers. Ramanujan continues: "I had just been converted by Russell to the 'scientific attitude'. I (and my generation) was troubled by his holding together in one brain both astronomy and astrology; I looked for consistency in him, a consistency he didn't seem to care about" (36). Ramanujan typified a generation of modern English-speakers that believed, as evidenced by his puzzlement at his father's behaviour, in the instrumentality of reason. Ramanujan's father's amazing versatility of personal philosophy, when post-structuralism was not heard of, cannot be explained.

"CO-RESPONDING"

Although Indian English fiction has long been a distinct area in literary studies, Indian English film is yet to receive scholarly attention. But in such academic exercises these genres are apt to be studied in isolation, that is, a work of fiction as a "literary text" and a film as another "text". It seems to me more sensible, if expedient, to look at the social phenomena of which they are part. Both genres have resulted from India's socio-historical experience of the reception and cultural dissemination of English. Both the genres derive from the culture of English, apart from corresponding with each other in ways explained in the foregoing chapters. Both of them *correspond* with and respond at once to that culture. In this study I have tried to show the nature and extent of such *correspondences* in select perspectives. Furthermore, I have studied fiction and film, basically *stories*, which are not always consciously ordered as history. While a story does not claim coherence and order, history is an interpreting device and advances coherence. I have tried to show how *English* strategically orders the incoherence of "stories" of our films and fiction as *history* of our post-globalisation.

English has brought about changes in the structures of such age-old Indian institutions as religion, community life and kinship. These changes are reflected by and presented in the films and fiction. Social and ethical morality has consistently grown more liberal and somewhat permissive. Family has become a smaller but powerful unit detached from the clan and caste systems that once determined it. Religious traditions, contrary to logic and expectations, have defined for themselves new roles in Indian society. For Indian English films and fiction sexuality has never been a taboo, or a means of commercial success, at least in general. (Shobha De perhaps and *Mumbai Matinee* certainly are exceptions.) In Indian English fiction and films sexuality is often, or apparently, a serious theme rather than a titillating diversion. Mira Nair's *Kama Sutra* in English was watched by academics, film critics and presumably mature audiences in metros, but its dubbed edition in Hindi was screened in B and C class cinemas in their usual semi-porn category.

Paro and *Socialite Evenings* are tales of sexual escapades and orgies of the metropolitan elite. The film *Split Wide Open* openly discusses adultery, sexual abuse and homosexuality as central themes. Because of the English language in which these films and fictions are made, such issues can expect to be treated seriously and with a certain degree of maturity. If one compares the treatment of lesbianism in *Girlfriend* (a Hindi film) and *Fire* (an Indian English film), the distinction would become much clearer. In the one, lesbianism is portrayed as a disease, a behavioural defect caused by traumatic childhood, whereas in the other it is shown as an alternative form of sexuality. The difference in the treatment of the same subject clearly illustrates the attitude inherent where English intervenes as the "medium". The sensible, serious and rational discussion of sexual abuse in *Monsoon Wedding* and *Split Wide Open* defines a new idiom in Indian cinema. In *Mumbai Matinee* and *English, August*, the heroes are sexually deprived young men whose thought (presumably formed by the English education) rebels against the restrictive social mores to which they are forced to conform. This proves that English provides a less restrictive venue for taboo subjects that otherwise would not be spoken about except in embarrassed, bashful and apologetic tones. My attempt here has been to read responses of this kind that Indian English fiction and films together make to the socio-cultural matrix sponsored by, or under the aegis of, English.

Today one often comes across families where the children speak only English. They are usually the children of interlingual marriages, as when one marries a person from another state. The very language of such a relationship is usually English (sometimes Hindi with English). Such marriages have been made possible by people's migration for educational and professional purposes to (usually) a metropolis where friendships turn into "affairs", and occasionally graduate into marriages. These marriages are a rejection of the traditional determinants such as religion, caste and language, and the adoption of emotional intimacy as the basis for forming a family. In such situations the ethos of the "modern" prevails against the traditional systems that allow for less personal choice and whose authorities are unquestioned because they are founded on kinship, antiquity, religion or language. These families, mostly confined to urban-industrial middle-class India, contribute children to a generation whose identity is not regional or linguistic, but collective and national. The name of a person today, unlike in earlier times, is no key to his ethnic background. Names like "Rahul", "Suresh", "Rohit" and "Bobby" make it impossible to distinguish a Punjabi from a Malayalee. The characters of fiction and films in English mostly bear such names. Many of them, due to the overwhelming attractiveness of a more "non-ethnic" name, anglicise their names: Agastya Sen into "August" (*English, August*), Krishnagopal Reddy into "Kris" (*American Desi*), Jesminder into "Jess" (*Bend It Like Beckham*) and so on.[2] The example of *Bollywood Calling* in Chapter 3 has briefly commented on a name like "Subrahmaniam", which can only suggest a stereotypical "provincial" comic character. The preference for a "modern" name is unambiguous in Indian English fiction and films. Such characters, the urban types with stylish short names, are most common all over the country today. That this generation, whose population, visibility, influence, power and promise are ever on the increase, is likely to decide the future of modern India is becoming increasingly certain. And importantly, this is a generation of Indians whose "primary" language is, for all intents and purposes, English, or an Indian language whose linguistic basis practically has become English.

The latter claim would have sounded more exaggerated than is really the case, were it not for the substantial evidence one might gather from the Hindi – and nearly all Indian language

– film promos and advertisements. It is not only the case that nearly all film persons in Bollywood are fluent and often effective communicators. English is their chosen medium. The VCD/ACD jackets of films released since the 1990s are in English, their design and appeal quintessentially English. Yash Chopra's

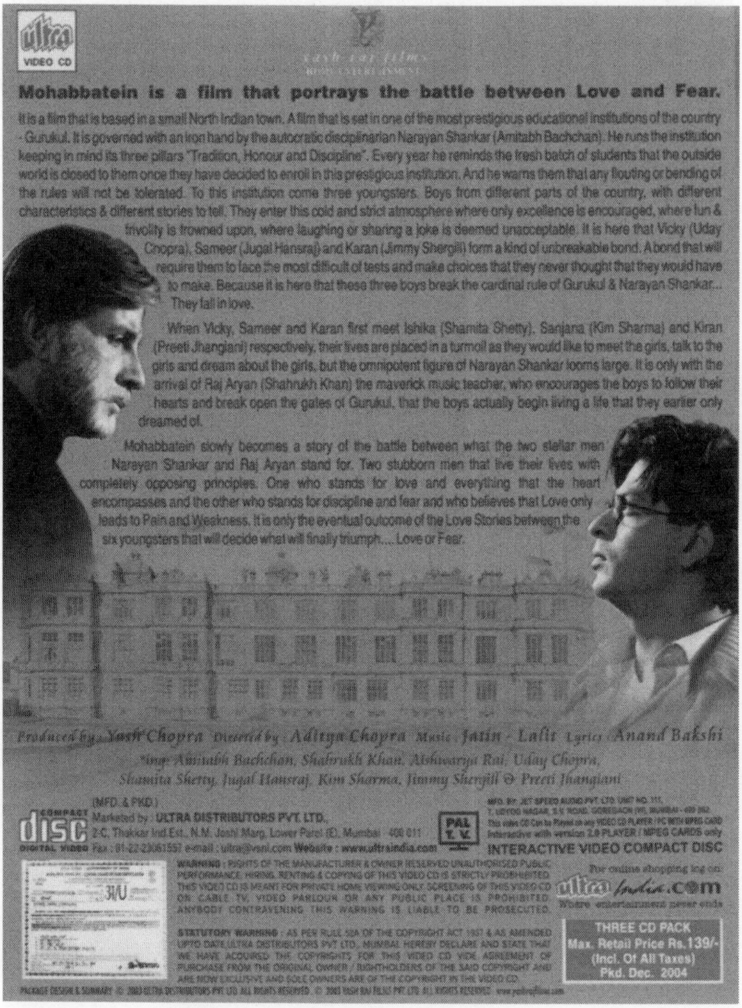

The film description on the *Mohabbatein* VCD cover

Mohabbatein, to take a random example, is subtitled "an Aditya Chopra film". There are interesting things to read here, if one were attentive to the social life of English in India. They include "correspondences" – those between film and fiction, Hindi and English, India and the West on the one hand, and the audio-visual semiotics of "filmi" fiction on the other. *Mohabbatein* (literally means loves!) proclaims the *amor-vincit-omnia* cliché of film and fiction through the loves of at least four pairs of lovers of various age-group against whom stands the sworn enemy of sexual love and courtship in the person of the Principal of a swanky, idyllic public school somewhere in the Doon valley (but really in Wiltshire, UK, the location where the film was shot. See the VCD cover image). Of course, the school is called "Gurukul" where the students are constantly made aware of our hoary traditions of discipline, learning, values, etc. Enter a music teacher with a violin. Everything changes. Love and physicality erupt as never before on the scene. The rest of *Mohabbatein* is all song and dance, and happy unions.

The advertisement of *Mohabbatein* is an extraordinary leaf off the book of Indian English semiosis. The poster and the VCD/ACD covers are in English. The pan-Indian audience can, however, read the title. What they cannot read is easily told them by the stills used for advertisement: Shah Rukh Khan and Aishwarya Rai in an affectionate embrace, Shah Rukh Khan playing a violin, etc. The sale of the album was nearly as huge as the success of the film in most theatres in India. There is, however, more to the advertisement imagery than all this fiddle. Maple leaves are strewn all over the picture – a slight visual foretaste of the leaves that swiftly collect and are blown away by autumn winds when the primary credits roll on the big screen. For the cognoscenti, the maple leaves and the fiddle/violin connect. The fiddle is made of maple wood, a connection school children in the West may readily make. Of course the

Amor-vincit-omnia

fiddle tutor plays chord-music on it, and there is very little "Indian" about either this liberated love or the philosophy he poses against the old Principal. A correspondent example will

Another "Gurukul"; VCD cover for the film *Rockford*

be the Indian English film *Rockford*, which not only has an English name but uses the same kind of visual imagery as *Mohabbatein*. The school buildings in both the film are alike, their architecture quintessentially English (see picture).

* * *

INDIA THROUGH ENGLISH

It is often thought incomprehensible that the most highly educated in India are the most religious, and it is often blamed on the vestiges of superstition. The confusion here is nothing but the invisibility of the apparent: among other things, religion has also become a matter of individual choice through an unenviable deployment of versatile reason. Belief, rituals and piety have become ways of socialisation, a type of psychological stimulant, a welcome opium for the people or an alternative recreation in the age of reason. The examples from Indian English fiction and films for such practices of "modern" religion are worth remembering here. Anjali taking to religion in *Socialite Evenings*, the Punjabi wedding rituals of *Monsoon Wedding*, the use of Krishna–Radha myth in *Let's Talk* are all cases in point.

English also helps us take a fresh-minded look at all that is handed down – Indian medicine, music, art, sculpture, architecture, flora and fauna, scholarly practices, etc. Their relocation to public auditoria, galleries, universities and research dissertations from the religious and caste-related contexts was indeed mediated through English, the driving force of modernity. English afforded us a new way of seeing, or configuring, India, a perspective unavailable to Indians in native languages through a massive defamiliarisation of culture – chiefly designated in the binaries as *desi* (indigenous) and *videsi* (western/non-native).

The history of India as a nation was wholly the result of the western discipline of historiography conceived in English. The most authoritative and respected histories of India are all in English. As I have suggested earlier, this may be because English is regarded as a more rational, factual, precise and perhaps rigorous medium. The style in which histories are written even today took shape in the "age of prose and reason". On the other hand, many an ancient and venerable Indian tradition has been created, as much as written, in English. In his book on globalisation, the British sociologist Anthony Giddens makes a remark valid enough for the Indian traditions as much as to the other similar traditions elsewhere: "Much of what we think of as traditional and steeped in the mist of time, is actually a product at most of the last couple centuries, and is often much more recent than that" (37). A controversial example will be the Hindu religion. On the world stage India was presented as a land of rich traditions and philosophy by English-speaking saints, gurus, teachers and swamis like Vivekananda, Aurobindo, Purohit Swamy, Tagore, Gandhi and Chinmayananda, and Ravi Shankar of recent vintage. Earlier I said that English is the future of India, and I will not be wrong to add now that it is also the past of India.

If we examine the register of anything that is written or filmed in English, we find that it tends towards the less locally bound, the general and the national – or even the international. There is an international inventory of ideas and images that one easily takes for granted in an Indian English speaker. This includes a required knowledge of historical events like the Renaissance, Enlightenment, the French revolution, the American revolution, the Third Reich (but not the "Sepoy Mutiny"); figures like Locke and Bentham, Washington and Lincoln, Gandhi or Hitler; films like *Gone with the Wind* and *Psycho*; writers like Shakespeare and Proust; Pele, the Beatles, Yassar Arafat, Saddam Hussain. We remember and recall English as history and history in English. The cosmopolitanism that is likely to characterise tomorrow's postnational (at least on paper) world is then already underway in India, and the Indian English films and fiction are where we find evidences for it.

In my view, today's Indian English fiction and film are a direct response to the newfound scheme of culture that I attribute to English. The war of the generations, switching to a more western lifestyle, the growing interest in global topics and being part of a global culture, and despite all this, gravitating all the more towards India's own traditions – these are the commonest themes of life in metropolitan India. These are also the stock themes of the Indian English fiction and films of our era. This correspondence makes them representative genres of metropolitan English-speaking India. Theirs is a "co-response", a consonant answering, to the English-mediated ways of contemporary Indian life.

"ENGLISH LIFE"

Indian English fiction and film become distinct from other Indian literatures and films, and akin to each other, because they depict the "English life" of India. When a language brings in a way of life, a new culture emerges. We have already studied in detail the emergence of the culture of English in Chapter 1. I have consistently argued that fiction and films in Indian English are an offshoot of this culture. Hence, they exclusively answer (and are answerable) to the culture of English, which makes the genres *correspondent*. This also means that English has become the most and only suitable language for fiction and films that intend to show a special way of life – the life of a section of urban India.

The foregoing chapters have detailed the "English life" as presented in Indian English fiction and films. In *36 Chowringhee Lane* we see the gentry of Calcutta speaking English and enthusiastically embracing "English" ways of life. The hero Samresh aspires to be a writer, wants to live in a colonial apartment, and has an unrestricted love-life with his girlfriend Nandita. The whole society shown in the film looks up to English – vintage English music, English literature, etc. – and hopes to boost its respectability by gaining more "Englishness". The film is faithful in answering to the social reality of "English Indians" who have set themselves apart from a bygone traditional India.

When one gets educated through English and grows up reading English books, one's membership in the class of English gets ensured. In Shobha De's *Socialite Evenings* and Upamanyu Chatterjee's *English, August*, the protagonists are of this upbringing. Karuna in *Socialite Evenings* is inspired by pulp fiction and becomes a model. Brought up in a rich household and steeped in English, Agastya Sen in *English, August* is indifferent to his administrative job in an obscure small town. These representatives of the urban youth yearn for cities and a glamorous life snubbing the lacklustre and mundane life of an earlier generation. The younger generation taking to new ways often leads to a conflict when their parents oppose it. But among the "English Indians" even that opposition is half-hearted, as we saw in films like *Bollywood/Hollywood* and *Bend It Like Beckham*. Both the films endorse the youth rebellion and show the parents to be supportive of them, although not without some initial resistance. The grandmother in *Bollywood/Hollywood* and the father in *Bend It Like Beckham* are examples of the new converts from an older generation.

The knowledge of English also makes possible a class migration. People who speak English gain a new respectability, and are looked up to by the society. Indian English fiction and films have amply documented this social reality. In *Split Wide Open* the young man K. P., despite being an orphan in the slums, interacts with the socialites and has friends among them because he can speak good English. As the Father in the film remarks, English gives one "the keys to the kingdom".

In our cities English often unites people of different mother tongues into one community. As a pan-national medium, it helps build friendships, associations, romances and marriages otherwise impossible because of language barriers. In other words, English catalyses cosmopolitanism. To take an example, in *English, August* we find a company of IAS officers and journalists. The surnames of each of them indicate a different regional identity. Agastya Sen must be a Bengali, Menon a Malayalee, and Govind Sathe, presumably a Marathi. Despite that, they have common subjects to have a spontaneous conversation. It is undoubtedly English that helps them avoid the Babel situation here.

The amount of information available (exclusively) through English is inexhaustible. The "global language" is also bound to bring with it global ideas and themes. The more one accesses and applies information through English, the more internationalised one's outlook becomes. Here is a random list of ideas, concepts and words that an "English Indian" would easily relate to: "calorie-conscious", "chartbuster", "matinee idol", "heartthrob", "fractured verdict", "secular fabric", "Spirit of Unity Concerts", "Apex Fares", "peasant revolt", "student visa", "Grammy Awards", "fitness freak", "disaster management", "spring–summer collection", "*The Prisoner of Azkaban*", "Sex and the City", "Incredible India", "Iranian film festival", "eco-tourism", "Mughal cuisine", "free home delivery", "*Hardtalk*", "spam mails", "Euro II emission norms", "hobbits", "national roaming", "Commonwealth literature", "roof garden", "DJ night" and "Gender Studies".

Salman Rushdie, Shobha De, Upamanyu Chatterjee, Jhumpa Lahiri, Bharti Mukherjee and Shashi Tharoor (and many more Indian writers in English I have not touched upon) freely borrow from an internationalised repertoire of ideas. Their audience in India or elsewhere would find it quite in tune with their own knowledge of international themes. Almost all Indian English films follow suit. In Chapters 3 and 4 we saw how the characteristic sensibility of "English India" is catered to by fiction and films in Indian English. The examples of films like *Bollywood Calling*, *Mumbai Matinee* and novels like *Show Business* prove the assumed superiority of the "English culture" over other cultures of India. As these examples show, it is now easy to categorise the society into two in terms of the opinions, preferences and tastes of the people. While one group would be the "English Indians", the other would comprise the rest of India. In other words, these films and fiction tell us unambiguously that there is a scale of social respectability and refinement that is proportionate to the extent of one's participation in what I have called the "English life" of India.

ENGLISH AND THE FACE OF URBAN INDIA

In the novel *English, August* Govind Sathe, a journalist, says, "... each language is an entire culture". He says this to condemn Indian English literature, which according to him doesn't really address the real India because it is in English. This episode is one example of the "otherness" fallacy that many are prone to when they think about Indian English. This fallacy results from assuming, believing or taking for granted that English is merely a foreign language and is an imposition. But the social life of English in India today proves that this assumption is purely superstitious. English has *in fact* taken roots and is bearing fruits. Because "each language is an entire culture", one must admit that Indian English too is an "entire culture".

That Indian English is a thriving culture has many proofs. Corporate India has made English into a customer product. Because advanced and key information for modern professions and life is available only in English, it has become a necessity and an embodiment of knowledge as power. "Information capitalism" in India is wholly reliant on its medium of English. It has thus become possible to "live English" with the heavy sponsorship of corporate India. English is an essential skill in the expanding job market of metropolitan corporate India. More and more young men and women of the country are encouraged to embrace English in order to "domesticate" them for the global business environment – the section about this phenomenon in the Introduction may be recalled here. In mega-malls, domestic flights, pubs, discotheques, lifestyle showrooms, internet chat rooms, bookshops and swanky cafés English is the de rigueur language. English accompanies all that is cherished by the young urban India. All this constitutes the grand national fantasy of English.

It may seem an overplaying of the importance of English to attribute all this to English alone. But the role of a language in shaping a culture is too important to play down. In the "world of English" just described, only people of a certain kind can enter. They are the affluent, educated city slickers whose culture can take any of these attributives: "modern", "unconventional", "secular", "cosmopolitan", "hybrid", etc. Their qualities, from body language to food habits, and dress code to choice of partners, are unambiguous and distinct from those of a previous generation. The source of this *ethos* may seem mysterious, and the cause of its uniform circulation in different parts of the country, inexplicable. The common factor, the organiser, or the conductor of this emergent culture has to be English, indirectly or directly. A well-organised and homogeneous culture is otherwise impossible without a language at its centre. The many evidences we have examined already from different forms of cultural expression (fiction, films, media, public ceremonies, etc.) seem to prove this unacknowledged or forgotten truth about English in India.

THE CYCLE OF CORRESPONDENCE

With the help of the term *correspondence* I also try to show the circularity of influence among fiction, film and society. That means looking at how films and fiction derive from social life, how fiction and film influence each other, and how they both in turn become reverse influences on life. My attempt is to demonstrate how this whole web of influcnces and communication is mediated through English. Many stock situations in Hindi films are widely parodied today – stories of brothers separated and reunited, revenge of father's murder, widowed mother, brigands kidnapping children and making them brigands, and daughter-in-law versus mother-in-law. Propagated by films, these ideas have become archetypes that people often apply in describing real-life situations. Films have become for people a frame of reference for their actual lives. Life is likened to and lived according to films. Today one finds the word "filmi" handier than ever to refer to actual events. *In turn*, this very phenomenon of the cinematisation of life becomes the subject of films – the Indian English films. Small wonder that English as the language of *reflection* (rational thought as well as mirroring of social reality) is also the language of self-*reflexive* cinema – *Bollywood Calling*, *King of Bollywood*, *Bollywood/Hollywood*, *Mumbai Matinee* and *Rang De Basanti*, for example. Indian English fiction has a corresponding list of novels by Shashi Tharoor, Sarnath Banerjee, et al. This self-reflexivity, which is the character of the times according to the post-modernists, is a typical feature of English-sponsored life in India.

I have argued in Chapter 4 that the unprecedented spread of visual culture has modified the written word. Literature quite often assumes the form of a visual-oriented narrative such as *Show Business*, *The Satanic Verses* and *Corridor*. The intrusion of the cinematic into many areas of life is to be seen as part of the worldwide "virtualisation" of life. The internet, television and other media have turned life into a colourful and stage-managed event. In India, English is the medium that pioneers these trends and organises the transformation. English is simply present behind each action and word in many a cinematic life. Thus the correspondences and influences *circulate*, that is, travel from life to film, from film to fiction, from fiction to news, cartoons, songs, advertisements completing a grand reciprocal mimesis.

THE SIGNIFICANCE OF CORRESPONDENCE

The correspondence between Indian English fiction and films becomes important for several reasons. Their medium is English, and they are two popular media of social opinion. The correspondence is occurring at the time when the social life of English in India is rapidly expanding. We may conclude that the English boom in our society is a necessary and now sufficient condition for our own fiction and films in English. I have focused on the post-1980s trends in fiction and film in Indian English, the period when they began to emerge as clearly correspondent in terms of cultures they replicate and feed on mutually. The successful career of English in India, which started in the first half of the nineteenth century with Macaulay's *Minutes*, has reached yet another turning point here. But the contemporary scene is far from simple. The current of globalisation and spread of telecommunication have made the fate of languages and culture very unpredictable. In India, they have secured the future of English. Today there is a strong sponsorship of English coming from public, private and corporate channels. The re-invention of English in the post-globalisation era has proved to be worth its while. The English culture of India is distinct and autonomous. English's adaptability has helped us forge a fresh approach to age-old Indian traditions.

The representative texts in prose fiction and films I have studied, I hope, provide with reliable clarity an understanding of the complex cultural role of English in the Indian multilingual context. As carriers of social comment, Indian English fiction and films are reliable guides to the social life of metropolitan

English as well. They both bear the same relationship to that social life and both respond similarly to it. These two genres represent the Indian English point of view. They are highly illustrative of the social image repertory sustained by English. They reveal the connection between contemporary visual culture in India and English language. They contribute significantly towards making Indian English one of the major world Englishes, like the British, Irish, American and Australian.

In the coming days English will have to be instrumental for the international presentation of the idea of India. Fiction and film can do this in a big way. As postindustrial societies will depend more on alternative forms of capital and power, English will prove infinitely handy for India to deal in commodities of culture. As the unacknowledged adhesive of the postnational world, English has more or less assured India's participation in the global future.

NOTES

1. This is true of characters not only on screen or in novels, but in reality too. The opponents of English like Laloo Prasad Yadav or hardcore right parties are increasingly reliant on English for propaganda and public visibility.
2. A shortened and anglicised name perhaps adds to the popular appeal of a celebrity. Film journalists in India were quick to pick up this habit from the Anglo-American pop-journalism which means Arnold Schwarzenegger by a simple "Arnie". For example, "Ash" for Aishwarya Rai, "Sush" for Sushmita Sen, "Maddie" for Madhavan, "SRK" for Shah Rukh Khan, "Big B" for Amitabh Bachan, etc.

Acknowledgements

I am thankful to Dr K. Narayana Chandran for his guidance in my research and for kindly agreeing to write the Foreword. I thank the University of Hyderabad for the research assistance. I owe a debt of gratitude to Mr Vinod Vasishtha, Managing Director of Viva Books, who generously supported my work on this book.

Mr Narendar Kumar of Viva helped me with his professional image editing; special thanks to him for the aesthetic cover design. Thanks to Ms Geeta Bist of Viva for skilfully touching up the Laloo caricature.

Picture acknowledgements: The pictures from the novel *Corridor* by Sarnath Banerjee on pages 79, 83 and 84 are reproduced with the permission of Penguin Books India. The photograph of Nehru announcing Gandhi's death © *The Hindu*; the article on Mallika Sherawat © *The Times of India*; promotional materials for the film *Mohabbatein* © Yash Raj Films and Ultra Videos; the VCD cover image for the film *Rockford* © Padmini Films and BIT Videos.

Works Cited

BOOKS AND OTHER PRINT SOURCES

Appadurai, Arjun. *Modernity at Large*. Minneapolis: U of Minnesota P, 1996.

Banerjee, Sarnath. *Corridor*. New Delhi: Penguin, 2004.

Barthes, Roland. "The Photographic Message." *Barthes: Selected Writings*. Ed. Susan Sontag. N. p.: Fontana, 1982. 194–210.

Bhatt, Mahesh. "Bollywood Meets Hollywood." *Span*, 61.2 (2003): 3–6.

Bourdieu, Pierre. Introduction. *Distinction: A Social Critique of the Judgement of Taste*. Trans. Richard Nice. London: Routledge, 1984. 1–7.

Braj Kachru, B. *The Alchemy of English*. Delhi: OUP, 1986.

Chatterjee, Upamanyu. *English, August: An Indian Story*. London: Faber, 1998.

Crystal, David. *English as a Global Language*. Cambridge: CUP, 1997.

Rev. of *Corridor*, by Sarnath Banerjee. *The Week* 22–26 (2004): 64.

Rev. of *Corridor*, by Sarnath Banerjee. Literary Review *The Hindu*. 30 May 2004: 5.

Dasgupta, Probal. *The Otherness of English: India's Auntie Tongue Syndrome*. New Delhi: Sage, 1993.

De, Aditi. "Through the Corridors of Life." Sunday Magazine *The Hindu* 30 May 2004: 5.

De, Shobha. *Socialite Evenings*. New Delhi : Penguin, 1988.

Derrida, Jacques. "Artifactualities." *Echographies of Television: Filmed Interviews*. By Derrida and Bernard Stiegler. Trans. Jennifer Bajorek. Cambridge: Polity, 2002. 1–27.

Ezekiel, Nissim. "Goodbye Party to Miss Pushpa T. S." *Collected Poems 1952–1988*. Delhi: Oxford, 1989. 190–191.

Fiedler, Leslie A. "The Death and Rebirth of the Novel." *The Theory of the Novel: New Essays*. Ed. John Halperin. New York: OUP, 1974. 189–209.

Genette, Gerard. *Narrative Discourse.* Ithaca: Cornell, 1980.

Ghose, Sagarika. "The Call Centre Drawl". *The New Indian Express* (Hyderabad Ed.) 4 June 2003: 8.

Giddens, Anthony. *Runaway World: How Globalisation Is Reshaping Our Lives*. London: Profile, 2002.

Gokhale, Namita. *Paro: Dreams of Passion*. London: Hogarth, 1984.

Krishnaswami, Revathi. "The Claims of Globalisation Theory: Some Contexts and Contestations." *South Asian Review*, 24.1 (2003): 18–32.

Kureishi, Hanif. "Introduction to *My Beautiful Laundrette*." *Dreaming and Scheming: Reflections on Writing and Politics*. London: Faber, 2002. 123–126

Lahiri, Jhumpa. *Interpreter of Maladies*. New Delhi: Harper Collins, 1999.

Mukherjee, Bharati. "Hindus." *Darkness*. Delhi: Penguin, 1990. 127–141

Narayan, R. K. "A Horse and Two Goats." *A Horse and Two Goats*. Delhi: Hind, 1970. 9–30.

Padmanabhan, Manjula. "The Copper-Tailed Skink." *Best Loved Indian Stories of the Century*. Eds. Indira Srinivasan, and Chetna Bhatt. Vol. 1. Delhi: Penguin, 1999. 195–209.

Quirk, Randolph. Foreword. *The Indianisation of English: The English Language in India*. By Braj B. Kachru. Delhi: OUP, 1983. vii.

Rajyadhyaksha, Ashish and Paul Willeman. *The Encyclopaedia of Indian Cinema*. New Delhi: OUP, 1995.

Ramanujan, A. K. "Is There an Indian Way of Thinking: An Informal Essay." *The Collected Essays of A. K. Ramanujan*. Ed. Vinay Dharwadker. New Delhi: OUP, 1999.

Rushdie, Salman. *Midnight's Children*. London: Jonathan Cape, 1981.

—. *The Satanic Verses*. London: Viking, 1988.

Sharma, Jyoti. "Viagra and the Nun." Delhi Times *The Times of India*. 11 Apr 2004: 1.

Tharoor, Shashi. *Show Business*. New Delhi: Viking, 1991.

—. "Things That Happen Only in India." Sunday Magazine *The Hindu*, 13 Aug 2006: 3.

Thussu, Daya Kishan. "The Hinglish Hegemony: The impact of Western Television on Broadcasting in India." *Television in Contemporary Asia*. Eds. David French and Michael Richards. New Delhi: Sage, 2000. 293–311.

Vaidyanathan, T. G. "Aparna Sen, *36 Chowringhee Lane* (1981)." *Hours in the Dark: Essays on Cinema*. Delhi: OUP, 1996. 109–113.

FILMS

American Desi. Dir. Piyush Dinkar Pandya. Prods. Piyush Dinkar Pandya, and Deep Katadre. Perf. Deep Katadre, Purva Bedi. Channel Nine, 2001.

Bend It Like Beckham. Dir. Gurinder Chadha. Prods. Gurinder Chadha, and Deepak Nayar. Perf. Parminder K. Nagra, Keira Knightley, and Jonathan Rhys Meyers. Fox Searchlight, 2002.

Bollywood Calling. Dir. Nagesh Kukunoor. Prod. B. Satyanarayana. Perf. Pat Cusick, Perizad Zorabian, Navin Nischol, and Om Puri. PNC, 2002.

Bollywood/Hollywood. Dir. Deepa Mehta. Prod. David Hamilton. Perf. Rahul Khanna, and Lisa Ray. Magnolia Pictures, 2002.

Everybody Says I'm Fine. Dir. Rahul Bose. Prod. Vivek Vaswani. Perf. Rehan Engineer, Koel Purie, Pooja Bhatt, and Rahul Bose. Insight Productions, 2002.

Hyderabad Blues. Dir., and Prod. Nagesh Kukunoor. Perf. Nagesh Kukunoor, and Rajashree Nair. Kukunoor Movies, 1998.

Let's Talk. Dir. Ram Madhvani. Prod. Vinod Iyer. Perf. Boman Irani, and Maia Katrak. Shift Focus, 2002.

Monsoon Wedding. Dir. Mira Nair. Prods. Caroline Baron, and Mira Nair. Perf. Naseeruddin Shah, Lillette Dubey, Shefali Shetty, and Vasundhara Das. Universal, 2001.

Mr and Mrs Iyer. Dir. Aparna Sen. Prod. Rupali Mehta, and N. Venkatesan. Perf. Konkana Sensharma, and Rahul Bose. Tips, 2002.

Mumbai Matinee. Dir. Anant Balani. Prod. Rangita Pritish Nandy. Perf. Rahul Bose, Perizad Zorabian, Vijay Raaz, and Saurabh Shukla. PNC, 2003.

Rockford. Dir. Nagesh Kukunoor. Prods. Elahe Hiptoola, Padmini Kolhapure, and Nagesh Kukunoor. Perf. Rohan Dey, Nandita Das, and Nagesh Kukunoor. 2000.

Split Wide Open. Dir. Dev Benegal. Prod. Anuradh Parikh. Perf. Rahul Bose, Ayesha Dharker, and Rajika Puri. Tropicfilm, 1999.

36 Chowringhee Lane. Dir. Aparna Sen. Prod. Shashi Kapoor. Perf. Jeniffer Kendal, Dhritiman Chatterjee, Debasree Roy. 1981.

INTERNET SOURCES

Ebert, Roger. Rev. of *Everybody Says I'm Fine*, dir. Rahul Bose. *Chicago Sun-Times* <http//www.suntimes.com/ebert/ebert_reviews/20 004/03/031202.html>

Rotten Tomatoes. <http//www.rottentomatoes.com/>

Strickland, Jon. Rev. of *Everybody Says I'm Fine*, dir. Rahul Bose. *LA Weekly*. <http//www.laweekly.com/f.../film_results.php?showid=2397&Submit.x=45&Submit.y=1>

Tharoor, Shashi. "Bedevilling Question of the Cadence of English." *The Hindu* 5 Aug 2001. <http://www.hindu.com/thehindu/2001/08/05/stories/13050676.htm>

The Internet Movie Database. <http//www.imdb.com/>

Welcome to India. <http://www.andrew.cmu.edu/user/gkumar/WelcomeToIndia.htm>

Index of Names

General Index